REBUILDER'S GUIDE

*"...Thou shalt raise up the foundations
of many [Godly] generations; and thou
shalt be called, The repairer of the breach,
The restorer of paths to dwell in."*

Isaiah 58:12

All Scripture references are from the King James Version of the Bible, unless otherwise noted.

Printed in the United States of America.

Fourteenth Printing, April 2005   040087

ISBN 09-16888-06-1

Library of Congress
Catalog Card Number: 80-80352

THE GOALS OF A REBUILDER

TO REBUILD A HEART THAT SEEKS AFTER GOD	**1**
TO REBUILD A COMMITMENT TO GOD'S DESIGN FOR MARRIAGE	**2**
TO REBUILD A CLEAR CONSCIENCE AND A FORGIVING SPIRIT	**3**
TO REBUILD THE MARRIAGE AS FAR AS SCRIPTURALLY POSSIBLE	**4**
TO REBUILD A LEARNING RELATIONSHIP WITH THE CHILDREN	**5**
TO REBUILD PAST FAILURES INTO AN EFFECTIVE LIFE MESSAGE	**6**
TO REBUILD THE MARRIAGES OF OTHERS WITH GOD'S TRUTH	**7**

TABLE OF CONTENTS

A REBUILDER IS . . .

- One who has purposed to seek God's best for his or her personal life, marriage, family, and ministry to others.

- One who is learning to see his circumstances from God's perspective rather than from his or her limited frame of reference.

- One who is committed to the seven basic goals of a rebuilder.

THE NAME REBUILDER . . .

- Presents a positive outlook. *viewpoint; expectation or prospect*

- Produces respect and admiration.

- *to urge into action; to inspire* Prompts fellowship and encouragement.

- Explains basic motivations and desires.

- Protects from wrong counsel.

- Establishes a standard of purpose.

- Causes wrong influences to leave.

A REBUILDER'S RESPONSE . . .

When asked if you are divorced: "My marriage failed, but now I am a rebuilder."

GOAL NUMBER **1**

REBUILDING A HEART THAT SEEKS AFTER GOD

". . . As long as he sought the Lord,
God made him to prosper."
                    II Chronicles 26:5

1 REBUILDER'S QUIZ

☐ ☐   1. Do you ever think about finding a new marriage partner?

☐ ☐   2. Do you evaluate people you know or meet on the basis of how they would be as a marriage partner?

☐ ☐   3. Did you spend time reading the Bible this morning?

☐ ☐   4. Did you put yourself to sleep last night by quoting Scripture in your mind to God?

☐ ☐   5. Do you ever fret against God because of what He allows to happen in your life?

☐ ☐   6. Do you relate your conflicts and counsel to Psalms and Proverbs?

☐ ☐   7. Have you spent at least one day in prayer and fasting during the past month?

☐ ☐   8. Have you ever been tempted and defeated even while you were praying for victory?

☐ ☐   9. Have you read at least one biography of a great Christian in the last six months?

☐ ☐   10. Can you quote the following chapters word perfect? Romans 6, Romans 8, James 1

☐ ☐   11. Are you active in and under the authority of a Bible-believing local church?

12. Do you give the first part of each pay-check to the Lord?

13. Do you ever have doubts as to whether or not you are a Christian?

14. Have you ever totally dedicated your life to God's will?

15. Are you expecting counsel and support from others that only God can give to you?

16. Do you have a respected friend who will keep you accountable to achieve these goals?

17. Do you have Scripture plaques or cards on the walls of your home?

18. Do you have a continual awareness that God is watching and weighing all your thoughts, words, and actions?

Answers are explained in the following pages.

SEEKING AFTER GOD MEANS . . .
EVALUATING MY TRUE MOTIVES

"I the Lord search the heart,
I try the reins, even to give every man according to his
ways, and according to the fruit of his doings."
Jeremiah 17:10

MY GOALS	WRONG MOTIVE	RIGHT MOTIVE
1. To seek after God	To repair my marriage	To make my ways pleasing to God
2. To be with mature Christians	To evaluate them as a possible marriage partner	To exhort each other to grow spiritually
3. To read the Bible daily	To obligate God to bless me	To discover the character of God and His ways
4. To meditate on Scripture every night	To get to sleep faster and to have peaceful sleep	To engraft Scripture into my soul so that it becomes a part of my daily decisions
5. To relate my experiences to Scripture	To focus on how others have been wrong	To see how I have been wrong and how I must change
6. To spend time in fasting and prayer	To lose weight and have better health	To increase my alertness to the Scriptural promptings of God's Spirit

7. To overcome temptations	To be free from spiritual conflict	To be strong in the Lord and fruitful for His glory
8. To read Christian biographies	To be encouraged by learning that they failed, too	To discover the disciplines that God used in making their lives fruitful
9. To memorize chapters of Scripture	To be able to quote them	To engraft them into my mind, will, and emotions
10. To get under God-given authority	To let others take the responsibility for my decisions	To confirm God's direction and avoid destructive temptations
11. To tithe from each paycheck	To have God bless my finances	To grow in faith and meet the needs of God's work
12. To have assurance of salvation	To never fear God's judgment	To go on to the deeper truths of the Christian life
13. To be totally dedicated to God's will	To make up for the failures in my past	To allow the power of Christ's Spirit to work through my life
14. To be accountable to others	To have them keep pressure on me	To remind me that I should be just as aware of my accountability to God
15. To put Scripture truths on my walls	To let others know that I'm seeking God	To be daily reminders of spiritual responsibility
16. To have a continual awareness that God is watching and weighing every thought, word, and action	To turn every conversation into "spiritual" talk	To grow in wisdom and to give others a hunger and thirst for God's truth

SEEKING AFTER GOD MEANS . . .
SPENDING TIME DAILY IN GOD'S WORD

"As newborn babes, desire the sincere milk of
the word, that ye may grow thereby."
I Peter 2:2

Become a person after God's own heart by translating your joys and sorrows through the Psalms. By reading five Psalms a day, you will not only complete the book of Psalms each month, but you will also be encouraged by how precise these Psalms are to your experience.

Learn the wisdom of God by reading, each day, the chapter of Proverbs which corresponds to the day of the month. Relate the Proverbs to the decisions and situations you face.

DAY	CHECK BOX WHEN READ	
1	☐ Psalms 1, 31, 61, 91, 121	☐ Proverbs 1
2	☐ Psalms 2, 32, 62, 92, 122	☐ Proverbs 2
3	☐ Psalms 3, 33, 63, 93, 123	☐ Proverbs 3
4	☐ Psalms 4, 34, 64, 94, 124	☐ Proverbs 4
5	☐ Psalms 5, 35, 65, 95, 125	☐ Proverbs 5
6	☐ Psalms 6, 36, 66, 96, 126	☐ Proverbs 6
7	☐ Psalms 7, 37, 67, 97, 127	☐ Proverbs 7
8	☐ Psalms 8, 38, 68, 98, 128	☐ Proverbs 8
9	☐ Psalms 9, 39, 69, 99, 129	☐ Proverbs 9
10	☐ Psalms 10, 40, 70, 100, 130	☐ Proverbs 10
11	☐ Psalms 11, 41, 71, 101, 131	☐ Proverbs 11
12	☐ Psalms 12, 42, 72, 102, 132	☐ Proverbs 12
13	☐ Psalms 13, 43, 73, 103, 133	☐ Proverbs 13
14	☐ Psalms 14, 44, 74, 104, 134	☐ Proverbs 14
15	☐ Psalms 15, 45, 75, 105, 135	☐ Proverbs 15
16	☐ Psalms 16, 46, 76, 106, 136	☐ Proverbs 16

SEEKING AFTER GOD MEANS . . .
LEARNING WHO GOD REALLY IS

*"The fear of the Lord is the
beginning of wisdom: and the knowledge
of the holy is understanding."*
Proverbs 9:10

God reveals Himself through His names. The more we understand His names and relate them to the needs and fears of our lives, the more we will enjoy God.

COMPOUND NAME OF GOD	MEANING OF NAME
1. Jehovah - jireh	I am God who provides a substitute for your salvation. (See Genesis 22:14.)
2. Jehovah - rophe	I am God who heals you. (See Exodus 15:26.)
3. Jehovah - nissi	I am God who leads to victory over immorality. (See Exodus 17:15.)
4. Jehovah - M'Kaddesh	I am God who sanctifies you. (See Leviticus 20:7-8.)
5. Jehovah - shalom	I am God who gives you peace. (See Judges 6:24.)
6. Jehovah - tsidkenu	I am God who teaches you justice. (See Jeremiah 23:5-6.)
7. Jehovah - rohi	I am God who cares for your daily needs. (See Psalm 23:1.)
8. Jehovah - shamma	I am God who is there. (See Ezekiel 48:35.)

CONTEXT OF GOD'S NAMES	APPLICATION
1. Jehovah-jireh (je-ho'-vah yeer'-he) *Literal: God who provides.* *Context: Genesis 22:1-14* God commanded Abraham to offer up his son, Isaac, as a burnt offering. Abraham and Isaac traveled for three days to get to the place that God had selected. Abraham built an altar and placed his son on it. As Abraham lifted his knife to slay his son, God stopped Abraham and instead provided a substitute—a ram caught in a thicket. "And Abraham called the name of that place Jehovah-jireh: as it is said to this day..." (Genesis 22:14).	My most cherished affection is I have fully surrendered this to God, so that He is free to take it anytime He wants ☐ Date If God takes what I cherish the most, am I trusting Him to replace it with what he knows is best? ☐ Yes ☐ No
2. Jehovah - rophe (je-ho'-vah ro'-phay) *Literal: God who heals.* *Context: Exodus 15:22-27* God had just led the nation of Israel out of the bondage of Egypt and through the Red Sea. After three days in the wilderness, they found no water; so they began to murmur. The Israelites then came to the waters of Marah, but they could not drink them because they were bitter. The Lord instructed Moses to cast a certain tree into the waters. When he did, they became sweet. Then God said, "...If thou wilt diligently hearken to the voice of the Lord thy God, and wilt do that which is right in his sight, ... I will put none of these diseases upon thee, which I have brought upon the Egyptians: for I am the Lord that healeth thee" (Exodus 15:26).	These irritations cause me to murmur The following people have tasted of my bitterness God wants me to accept the following "cross" so that He can heal others through me

17

CONTEXT OF GOD'S NAMES	APPLICATION

3. Jehovah - nissi (je-ho'-vah nis-see)
Literal: The Lord is my banner.
Context: Exodus 17

The nation of Israel continued to murmur against the Lord in the wilderness. Then the nation of Amalek came out to fight against them. The Amalekites were immoral and evil people. They are representative of immorality. God declared perpetual war against them. While Israel fought against Amalek, Moses went up to the hill. Whenever he held up his hands, Israel prevailed. When he let his hands down, Amalek prevailed. Aaron and Hur held up Moses' hands and Israel defeated the Amalekites. "And Moses built an altar, and called the name of it Jehovah-nissi" (Exodus 17:15).

I am aware that I am in a perpetual battle against the lusts of the flesh.
☐ Yes   ☐ No

I realize that I cannot fight this battle alone.
☐ Yes   ☐ No

☐ I purposed to lift up "holy hands" in prayer continually. (See I Timothy 2:8.)

I have asked the following two people to support me in daily prayer.

_____

_____

4. Jehovah-M'Kaddesh (je-ho'vah m'-kad'-desh)
Literal: I am the Lord which sanctifies you.
Context: Leviticus 20:7-8

God brought the nation of Israel to Mount Sinai. Moses went into the mountain and received the Ten Commandments from the hand of God. Then God instructed Moses to explain His laws and statutes to the entire nation of Israel. Within that instruction is the command, "Sanctify yourselves therefore, and be ye holy: for I am the Lord, your God, and ye shall keep my statutes, and do them: I am the Lord which sanctify you" (Leviticus 20:7-8).

☐I realize that God requires one to be holy. (See I Peter 1:16.)

☐ I also realize that it is not humanly possible for me to be perfect.

☐As a Christian, I am a part of Christ's spiritual body. This means that, as a part of Christ, I fulfilled all of the law's demands, and now He is living in me to do His will.

5. **Jehovah-shalom** (je-ho'-vah shal-lom')

> *Literal: The Lord send peace.*
> *Context: Judges 6:1-24*

The nation of Israel did evil in the sight of the Lord and the Lord delivered them into the hand of the nation of Midian for seven years. During harvest time, the Midianites came against Israel to steal all their crops. An angel of God appeared to Gideon and called him to deliver Israel from the oppression of the Midianites. When Gideon realized that he had seen an angel of the Lord, he was fearful. "And the Lord said unto him, Peace be unto thee; fear not; thou shalt not die. Then Gideon built an altar there unto the Lord, and called it Jehovah-shalom . . ." (Judges 6:23-24).

The chastening of God is upon Christians today in the following ways:
☐ enslavement to habits
☐ marriage breakdowns
☐ broken families

God is calling me to be a peacemaker in the following conflicts:

_____
_____
_____

6. **Jehovah-tsidkenu** (je-ho'-vah tsid-day'-noo)

> *Literal: The Lord our Righteousness.*
> *Context: Jeremiah 23:1-6*

The nation of Israel continued to rebel against the Lord and seek after other gods. God raised up prophets of His coming judgment. Jeremiah predicted that God would scatter the nation of Israel into all the corners of the earth, and then God would raise up a king from the line of David. In the last days He would gather the remnants of Israel and bring them back to their own lands. God's king would then execute judgment and justice in the earth. "In his days Judah shall be saved, and Israel shall dwell safely: and this is his name whereby he shall be called, THE LORD OUR RIGHTEOUSNESS" (Jeremiah 23:6).

☐ I realize that any law system that violates God's just standards will bring judgment to the nations and individuals who follow them.

☐ I purpose to delight myself in the law of the Lord so that I can seek His kingdom and His righteousness (justice) first. (See Matthew 6:33.)

CONTEXT OF GOD'S NAME	APPLICATION

7. Jehovah-rohi (je-ho'-vah ro'-ee)
   Literally: The Lord my shepherd.
   Context: Psalm 23:1;
   *   II Samuel 15:13–37*
When Absalom rebelled against his
father, David had to leave his home
and city. David and his faithful
followers fled over the Brook Kidron,
up the Mount of Olives, into the
plains of the wilderness of Judah, and
finally over the Jordan River. It was
during this time of rejection, disgrace,
public humiliation, lack of provisions,
and an uncertain future that David
wrote the twenty-third Psalm. The
calamity of his circumstances adds
majesty and meaning to the picture of
God as our shepherd.

☐ I have purposed to ac-
cept my present circum-
stances as an opportunity
for God to be my shepherd.

☐ My concern will not be
for my reputation, but "for
His name's sake."

☐ I will rejoice in God's
chastening as an evidence
of His love and presence.

☐ I will trust God to provide my daily needs.

8. Jehovah-shamma (je-ho-vah
   sham'-mah)
   Literally: The Lord is there.
   Context: Ezekiel 48:35
During the time and ministry of
Ezekiel, God revealed the future
restoration of Israel. In one of his
visions, Ezekiel described the city of
Jehovah. In that coming day when God
sets up His Kingdom and He Himself
dwells in Jerusalem, the new "... name
of the city from that day shall be, The
Lord is there" (Ezekiel 48:35).

☐ I realize that loneliness
results when I try to ar-
range circumstances around
my goals rather than for
God's glory.

☐ When times of discour-
agement and disappoint-
ment come, I will remem-
ber that I am an impor-
tant part of a much larger
program and that my trials
are not worthy to be com-
pared to the future glory
that God will give.

SEEKING AFTER GOD MEANS . . .
ENTERING INTO THE RESURRECTION POWER OF CHRIST

*"That I may know him, and the power of his resurrection,
and the fellowship of his sufferings,
being made conformable unto his death."*
Philippians 3:10

SEVEN STEPS TO ENTER INTO CHRIST'S POWER

1. Engraft Romans 6 and 8 into your soul

What does it mean to "engraft"?

To engraft Scripture into our souls means to make it a living extension of our lives so that it can produce spiritual fruit. The more Scripture we engraft into our souls, the more types of spiritual fruit we will have in our lives. If we engraft I Corinthians 13 into our souls, we will have the fruit of genuine love. If we engraft I Peter into our souls, we will have the fruit of patience during suffering. If we engraft Romans 6 and 8 into our souls, we will have victory over sin.

As branches are engrafted into a wild apple tree . . .

FREEDOM   FROM HABITS

*How does engrafting
the Word begin?*

. . . Scripture can be engrafted into our mind, will, and emotions.

The first step to engraft Scripture is to memorize a section word for word.

Romans 6

1. "What shall we say then? Shall we continue in sin, that grace may abound?

2. God forbid. How shall we that are dead to sin, live any longer therein?

3. Know ye not, that so many of us as were baptized into Jesus Christ were baptized into his death?

4. Therefore we are buried with him by baptism into death: that like as Christ was raised up from the dead by the glory of the Father, even so we also should walk in newness of life.

5. For if we have been planted together in the likeness of his death, we shall be also in the likeness of his resurrection:

6. Knowing this, that our old man is crucified with him, that the body of sin might be destroyed, that henceforth we should not serve sin.

7. For he that is dead is freed from sin.

8. Now if we be dead with Christ, we believe that we shall also live with him:

9. Knowing that Christ being raised from the dead dieth no more; death hath no more dominion over him.

10. For in that he died, he died unto sin once: but in that he liveth, he liveth unto God.

11. Likewise, reckon ye also yourselves to be dead indeed unto sin, but alive unto God through Jesus Christ our Lord.

12. Let not sin therefore reign in your mortal body, that ye should obey it in the lusts thereof.

13. Neither yield ye your members as instruments of unrighteousness unto sin: but yield yourselves unto God, as those that are alive from the dead, and your members as instruments of righteousness unto God.

14. For sin shall not have dominion over you: for ye are not under the law, but under grace.

15. What then? shall we sin, because we are not under the law, but under grace? God forbid.

16. Know ye not, that to whom ye yield yourselves servants to obey, his servants ye are to whom ye obey; whether of sin unto death, or of obedience unto righteouness?

17. But God be thanked, that ye were the servants of sin, but ye have obeyed from the heart that form of doctrine which was delivered you.

18. Being then made free from sin, ye became the servants of righteousness.

19. I speak after the manner of men because of the infirmity of your flesh: for as ye have yielded your members servants to uncleanness and to iniquity unto iniquity; even so now yield your members servants to righteousness unto holiness.

20. For when ye were the servants of sin, ye were free from righteousness.

21. What fruit had ye then in those things whereof ye are now ashamed? for the end of those things is death.

22. But now being made free from sin, and become servants to God, ye have your fruit unto holiness, and the end everlasting life.

23. For the wages of sin is death; but the gift of God is eternal life through Jesus Christ our Lord.

2. Picture yourself dead to sin

God's Word states that we are dead to sin.

Regardless of our own feelings to the contrary, God wants us to "reckon" ourselves dead indeed unto sin. To "reckon" is to count it to be so. In reality, what would this mean? If a dead man were propped up against a wall and a seductive woman were to walk in front of him, he would not even blink an eye. This is precisely the response that God wants us to have to the power and appeal of sin.

When did we die to sin?

We died to sin when we became a Christian. At that moment, we became part of Christ. Since we are a part of Christ, we share in all of His past achievements. When He was crucified, we were crucified with Him: "I am crucified with Christ . . ." (Galatians 2:20). When He was buried, we were buried: "Therefore we are buried with Him by baptism into death . . ." (Romans 6:4). When Christ rose from the dead, we rose from the dead: "If ye then be risen with Christ . . ." (Colossians 3:1).

3. Compare the law of sin to the law of gravity

It is one thing to say that we are dead to sin. It is quite a different matter to experience it. Yet this is precisely what God wants us to do on a continuing basis. We can do this by picturing the law of sin as the law of gravity and the law of the Spirit as the principle of aerodynamics.

Picture an eagle soaring in the air.

If that eagle folded in its wings, it would begin falling to the ground because the law of gravity would take over. A law is a law because it always operates the same way under the same conditions.

All that the eagle must do to stop falling is to stretch out its wings. The air rushing over its wings sets up a new force. It is the principle of aerodynamics. This principle is greater than the law of gravity. It does not annihilate the law of gravity; it overcomes it.

If we stop meditating in the face of a temptation, we will begin to fall. Falling is a very real experience. It does not take very many seconds to be defeated.

God designed the eagle to soar in the air and God designed the Christian to speak His truth in his heart day and night. God tells us to pray without ceasing (see I Thessalonians 5:17), to meditate on His truth day and night (see Psalm 1), and to speak the truth in our hearts (see Psalm 15:2).

This weaving of the Word into our thoughts is equivalent to the Hebrew phrase of "waiting upon the Lord." God promises that as long as we meditate on His truth, we will soar above the power of temptations. "But they that wait upon the Lord . . . shall mount up with wings as eagles . . ." (Isaiah 40:31).

Satan wants us to believe that when we start falling, there is nothing that we can do but surrender to the temptation. However, all we need to do is to stretch out those spiritual wings by quoting Romans 6. "What shall we say then? Shall we continue in sin . . . ." In a few moments the temptation will lose its power and appeal, and we will once again soar above temptation. In this way, the law of the Spirit of life in Christ Jesus lifts us up above the law of sin and death. (See Romans 8:2.)

Why it is fruitless to pray for victory:

One of Satan's favorite tricks is to get us to pray for victory while we are falling into temptation. The prayer is not very effective because it is not based on Scriptural truth. God does not want us to pray for victory. He wants us to enter into the victory that He has already provided in Christ. We were part of Christ's victory when we died and rose again with Him.

Why we must meditate the moment that we are tempted:

Just as the eagle has only a few seconds to stretch out its wings before falling to the ground, so we have only a few moments to visualize Romans 6 before we fall into temptation.

4. Personalize the truth of Romans 6

Part of the process of engrafting Scripture is turning it into a first-person prayer. As soon as you have a thorough grasp of Romans 6, begin to quote it to the Lord in the following way:

> *"What shall I say then? Shall I continue in sin that grace may abound? God forbid! How shall I, being dead to sin, live any longer therein? Don't I know that when I was baptized into Christ I was baptized into His death . . . ."*

After personalizing this Scripture, there is one more important step to follow. It is identifying the particular temptation that Satan would bring to us. Rather than using the word "sin," name the temptation. For example, if you are tempted to lust, quote:

> *"What shall I say then? Shall I continue to lust that grace may abound? God forbid! How shall I, being dead to lust, live any longer therein . . . ."*

If you are tempted to be bitter, quote:

> *"What shall I say then? Shall I continue to be bitter that grace may abound? God forbid! How shall I, being dead to bitterness, live any longer therein . . . ."*

5. Make no provision for the flesh

If we desire Christ's victory over a particular temptation, but we have provided the means to continue that temptation, we are only deceiving ourselves.

God commands us: "But put ye on the Lord Jesus Christ, and make not provision for the flesh, to fulfil the lusts thereof" (Romans 13:14).

This means that we must cleanse our lives and our homes of every item that grieves the Holy Spirit and contributes to spiritual defeat.

PROVISIONS FOR THE FLESH	DATE REMOVED
1. TV programs that present humanistic philosophies and sensuality.	_____
2. Music that violates God's standards.	_____
3. Sensual books and magazines.	_____
4. Habit-forming drugs and drink.	_____
5. Occult material.	_____
6. Friends who influence you to violate God's standards.	_____
7. Objects which have evil or improper associations.	_____
8. Clothing which defrauds.	_____
9. _____	_____

6. Become accountable for consistency

Go to those who are spiritually responsible for you, such as your parents, your partner, church leaders, or mature Christian friends, and ask them if they would regularly check up on your progress toward spiritual achievement. Tell them what your spiritual goals are and give them precise questions which they can ask you.

MY SPIRITUAL GOALS	ACCOUNTABILITY QUESTIONS
1. To engraft Scripture into my soul.	I would like to hear the Scripture that you have memorized during the past week.
2. Daily Bible reading.	What did you get from your Bible reading this morning?
3. Meditating on Scripture while going to sleep.	What Scripture did you use to put yourself to sleep last night?
4. Claiming Christ's victory over temptation.	Did you quote Romans 6 the last time you were tempted, and did you overcome the temptation?

7. Be Alert and Obedient to Promptings Which Are in Harmony with Scripture

It is not enough to reckon ourselves dead to sin. We must also be alive to the leading of the Holy Spirit. This means that we learn how to discern the promptings of God's Spirit and then quickly obey them. God's promptings will always be consistent with God's Word. He will never tell us to do something which is contrary to Scripture.

How do we become alert?

One of the most effective ways to increase our spiritual alertness is through prayer and fasting. As we set aside meal times or days in which to concentrate on the Word and prayer instead of eating, our spiritual alertness greatly increases.

How do we obey?

In Romans 6, we are told to obey the promptings of the Holy Spirit in the same way we obeyed the promptings of our sinful nature: "As ye have yielded your members servants to uncleanness and to iniquity unto iniquity; even so now yield your members servants to righteousness unto holiness" (Romans 6:19).

STEPS IN YIELDING TO SIN	STEPS IN YIELDING TO GOD
1. We experienced a sensual desire (e.g., to look at a sensual picture or television program).	1. We experience a Scriptural prompting (e.g., to invite someone for a meal, or to acknowledge when we are wrong).
2. We visualized the sensual pleasure that we would receive from this act.	2. We visualize the action required to obey this prompting.
3. We made the decision to fulfill our sensual desire.	3. We make a decision to obey the prompting.
4. We became the servant of sin. "Know ye not, that to whom ye yield yourselves servants to obey, his servants ye are . . ." (Romans 6:16).	4. Our decision confirms that we are God's servants.
5. We yielded the members of our body to carry out the sensual pleasure (our hands to pick up the pornographic material or turn on the television, our eyes to look at the lewd material, our minds to imagine further evil).	5. We yield the members of our body to carry out God's prompting (we use our mouth to invite someone for a meal, our hands to prepare it). (See Romans 12:1-2.)

SEEKING AFTER GOD MEANS . . .
BEING CONSISTENT WHEN WE DO NOT FEEL LIKE IT

"And let us not be weary in well doing: for in due season we shall reap, if we faint not."
Galatians 6:9

1. Building consistency with vows

Sometimes a married person does not feel like being married. That is one of the benefits of the marriage vow. It commits a person to being faithful during times of discouragement and disillusionment.

Sometimes a Christian does not feel like being spiritual. That is one of the benefits of making a vow to read the Bible for at least five minutes every day. That vow will carry you through times when you do not feel like being consistent in your walk with the Lord.

A rebuilder will only be successful if he or she builds respect and loyalty for a daily time with the Lord.

There will be the "ups" and "downs." There will be days when Bible reading will be like medicine—you take it because it is good for you. Other days the Bible will be like a bowl of cereal—dry but nourishing. Then there will be the days in which Bible study will be like apple pie and ice cream—the dessert to a special feast.

Behind much of this fluctuation of spiritual dullness, dryness, and fulfillment are "cycles of life."

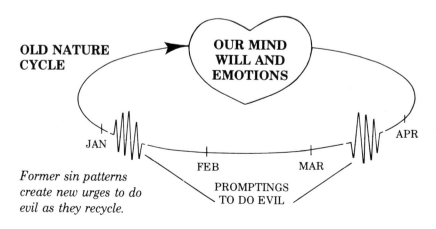

OLD NATURE CYCLE

OUR MIND WILL AND EMOTIONS

JAN   FEB   MAR   APR

Former sin patterns create new urges to do evil as they recycle.

PROMPTINGS TO DO EVIL

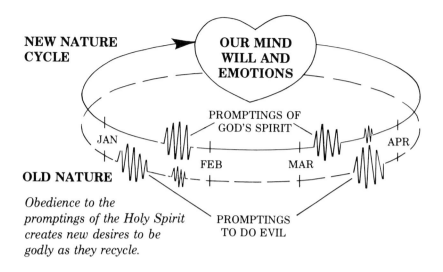

NEW NATURE CYCLE

OUR MIND WILL AND EMOTIONS

PROMPTINGS OF GOD'S SPIRIT

JAN FEB MAR APR

OLD NATURE

Obedience to the promptings of the Holy Spirit creates new desires to be godly as they recycle.

PROMPTINGS TO DO EVIL

2. Understanding the cycles of life

Every day we experience temptations to fulfill fleshly desires. Each time we obey a prompting, we imprint a sin pattern in the cycle of our lower nature.

When this pattern recycles in a day or week or month or year, it triggers a new prompting to repeat the fleshly desire. Each time the prompting is obeyed, it deepens and lengthens the sin pattern. Soon the pattern becomes a sinful habit.

When we become a Christian, we enter into Christ's victory over these old sin patterns and habits. God gives us a new nature. This new nature is responsive to the promptings of the Holy Spirit to claim our victory in Christ. Each time we obey the Holy Spirit's prompting, we develop or deepen spiritual patterns.

The goal of the Christian life is to build these spiritual patterns into a continuous sequence so that each time they are recycled through our soul, they will prompt us to be obedient and victorious in our daily walk with the Lord.

God breaks the power of our old nature at salvation and cleanses us from all sin. However, there is still the "pull" of the "law of sin" which Paul explains in Romans 6–8. This law of sin is pictured here in the form of cycles.

If a spiritual pattern is not as strong as the old sin pattern, we will experience spiritual dullness in Bible reading.

If a spiritual pattern is as strong as the old sin pattern, we will experience spiritual dryness in Bible reading.

If a spiritual pattern is stronger than the old sin pattern, we will experience spiritual delight in Bible reading.

SEEKING AFTER GOD MEANS . . .
HONORING THE LORD'S DAY

*"If thou turn away thy foot from the sabbath, from doing thy
pleasure on my holy day . . . then shalt thou delight thyself in the Lord;
and I will cause thee to ride upon the high places of the earth . . ."*
Isaiah 58:13-14

How do we honor the Lord's Day?

- "Not doing thine own ways" (Isaiah 58:13)—not doing your normal work, but making it a day of rest.
- "Nor finding thine own pleasure"—including amusement, entertainment, and self-seeking fulfillment.
- "Nor speaking thine own words"—engaging in frivolous conversation or meaningless talk.
- By realizing the Lord's Day begins the evening before. (See Genesis 1:5.)
- By entering into the teaching, fellowship, self-examination, and prayer with other Christians in a Bible-believing church. (See Hebrews 10:24-25.)
- By setting aside special time to be alone in God's Word. (See II Timothy 2:15.)
- By fasting and praying as God leads. (See Isaiah 58:6.)
- By entering into special Christian service to advance the kingdom of God, including giving your tithes. (See Malachi 3:10; I Corinthians 16:2.)
- By making it a day of spiritual refreshment and physical restfulness. (See Isaiah 58:14.)

SEEKING AFTER GOD MEANS . . .   7

(List further insights as God reveals them to you)

_____

_____

_____

_____

_____

_____

_____

_____

_____

_____

_____

_____

_____

_____

_____

_____

I have contacted the following persons to hold me accountable for
these spiritual goals:

     Name _____ Phone _____

     Name _____ Phone _____

     Name _____ Phone _____

Personal Commitment and Accountability

In rebuilding a heart that seeks after God:

☐ 1. I have purposed not to think about finding a new marriage partner.

☐ 2. I have purposed not to evaluate the people I meet on the basis of how they would be as a marriage partner.

    ☐ *The last time I was tempted to violate this, I effectively quoted Romans 6*

☐ 3. I have purposed to read the Bible every morning.

☐ 4. I have purposed to put myself to sleep every night by quoting Scripture in my mind to God.

    During the past month I have:

    ☐ *Read the Bible every morning.*

    ☐ *Quoted Scripture every night.*

☐ 5. I have purposed to thank God for what He allows to happen in my life.

☐ 6. I have purposed to relate my conflicts to the comfort and counsel of Psalms and Proverbs.

    During the past month I have:

    ☐ *Read through the book of Psalms.*

    ☐ *Read through the book of Proverbs.*

☐ 7. I have purposed to fast and pray on a regular basis.

☐ 8. I have purposed to identify with Christ's victory whenever I am tempted.

    During the past month I have:

    ☐ *Fasted and prayed at least one day.*

    ☐ *Experienced victory over temptation by quoting Romans 6 when tempted.*

☐ 9. I have purposed to get acquainted with great men and women in God's "Hall of Fame."

☐ 10. I have purposed to engraft key portions of Scripture into my soul.

    During the past month I have:

☐ *Started reading a Christian biography.*

☐ *Started engrafting Romans 6–8 into my soul.*

☐ 11. I have purposed to become active in and under the authority of a Bible-believing local church.

☐ 12. I have purposed to honor God by returning to Him the first portion of my income.

    During the past month I have:

☐ *Regularly attended church.*

☐ *Given my tithe to the local church.*

☐ 13. I have put my trust in the finished work of the Lord Jesus Christ for my salvation.
Date

☐ 14. I have totally dedicated my body to God as a living sacrifice to accomplish His will.
Date

☐ 15. I have purposed not to expect counsel or support from others before first seeking it from God.

☐ 16. I have purposed to become accountable to a trusted person in order to achieve and maintain these goals.

    During the past month I have:

☐ *Sought counsel from God first.*

☐ *Established a program of accountability with a mature person.*

☐ 17. I have purposed to put Scripture on the walls of my home.

☐ 18. I have purposed to become consciously aware of the fact that God is watching and evaluating every thought, word, and action.

    During the past month I have:

☐ *Posted Scripture verses on my walls.*

☐ *Become aware that God is watching me.*

GOAL NUMBER **2**

REBUILDING A COMMITMENT TO GOD'S DESIGN FOR MARRIAGE

"For this cause shall a man leave his father and mother, and shall be joined unto his wife, and they two shall be one flesh. This is a great mystery: but I speak concerning Christ and the church."

Ephesians 5:31-32

REBUILDER'S QUIZ

True   False

1. Marriage begins with a physical union, not just the marriage ceremony.

2. If one partner commits adultery, the other partner is free to end the marriage.

3. Desertion by one marriage partner is also Scriptural grounds for ending the marriage.

4. The Scriptural right to divorce carries with it the right to remarry.

5. If one partner divorces and remarries, the other partner is then free to remarry.

6. If your partner wants a divorce, you should not contest it.

7. A marriage in which there is continual conflict and lack of love should not be required to continue.

8. People should forgive and forget the sin of a repentant adulterer in the same way they do a repentant thief.

9. As long as both partners agree, any type of physical affection is proper in marriage.

10. With today's pressures, a husband and wife should share equal authority in the family.

11. As the head of the house, the husband should look only to God in making his decisions.

See answers on page 67.

GOD DESIGNED MARRIAGE TO ILLUSTRATE:

GOD'S RELATIONSHIP WITH ISRAEL

GOD'S DEALINGS WITH ISRAEL	RELATIONSHIP TO MARRIAGE
1. God chose Abraham and made an unbreakable covenant with him. (See Genesis 17:2.)	Marriage begins with an unbreakable covenant between husband and wife. (See Romans 7:2.)
2. Israel made many mistakes, but God was very patient with her. (See Psalm 118:2.)	A husband and wife must be very patient and forgiving toward each other. (See Colossians 3:19.)
3. God reaffirmed His covenant with Israel on many occasions. (See Exodus 6:5; Leviticus 26:42.)	A husband and wife should reaffirm their love and commitment to each other on many occasions. (See Proverbs 5:19.)
4. Israel became prosperous and complacent and soon lost her love for God. (See Deuteronomy 6:12.)	A husband or wife must never lose their sense of needing each other or they will lose their love for each other. (See Proverbs 31:11.)
5. Israel committed adultery against God after comparing God's leadership with the gods of other nations. (See Exodus 20:3; Psalm 78:56-61.)	No matter how ideal your partner is, there is a danger of becoming discontent by comparing your partner with others. (See Proverbs 2:16.)
6. God is patiently waiting for Israel to return to Him. Meanwhile, He is concentrating on the engagement of His Son to the Church. (See Romans 11:11.)	If a partner should leave, the other partner should remain single and concentrate on the spiritual growth of the children. (See I Corinthians 7:11; Malachi 2:13-16.)

GOD DESIGNED MARRIAGE TO ILLUSTRATE:

GOD'S REDEMPTION OF MANKIND

THE JEWISH WEDDING	RELATIONSHIP TO SALVATION
1. The prospective bridegroom took the initiative and traveled from his father's house to the home of the prospective bride.	Christ left His Father's house and came to earth to gain a bride for Himself. (See Ephesians 5:25-28.)
2. The father of the woman then negotiated with the prospective bridegroom the price that must be paid to purchase his bride (groom's financial responsibility).	Christ had to pay the price with His own blood. (See I Corinthians 6:19-20.)
3. When the bridegroom paid the purchase price, the marriage covenant was thereby established. At that point, the man and woman were regarded to be husband and wife, even though no physical union had taken place.	The believer has been declared to be sanctified or set apart exclusively for Christ. (See Ephesians 5:25-27.)

4. The moment the covenant was established, the bride was declared to be set apart exclusively for the bridegroom. The groom and the bride then drank from a cup over which the betrothal benediction had been pronounced. This symbolized that the covenant relationship had been established.

Christ symbolized this marriage covenant through communion at the Last Supper. (See I Corinthians 11:25.)

5. After the marriage covenant was in effect, the groom left the home of the bride and returned to his father's house. He remained there for a period of twelve months separated from his bride.

Christ returned to His Father's house following the payment of His purchase price. (See John 6:62.)

6. During this period of separation, the bride gathered her wardrobe and prepared for married life. The groom prepared living accommodations in his father's house for his bride.

Christ is preparing a place for His bride and is also sending pastors and teachers to perfect the bride for the coming wedding. (See John 14:2; Ephesians 4:11-13.)

7. After this period of separation, the groom, best man, and other male escorts left the house of the groom's father, usually at night, and conducted a torch-light procession to the house of the bride.

Christ will soon come from His Father's house in heaven accompanied by an angelic host. (See John 14:3.)

8. The bride was expecting her groom to come for her; however, she did not know the exact time. Thus, the groom's arrival was preceded by a shout.

Christ's return will be preceded by a shout. (See I Thessalonians 4:16.) We expect His return, but we do not know the day or the hour.

THE JEWISH WEDDING	RELATIONSHIP TO SALVATION
9. The groom received the bride with her female attendants and returned to his father's house.	The bride will be caught up with the Lord to be with Him. (See I Thessalonians 4:14-17.)
10. The bride and groom then entered the bridal chamber and, in the privacy of that place, entered into physical union for the first time, thereby consummating the marriage.	Christ's union with the Church will take place in heaven for all eternity. (See I Thessalonians 4:17.)

When we grasp the fact that the entire plan of redemption is so precisely illustrated by the Jewish wedding, we will clearly see that there is no place for divorce after marriage. Its parallel in redemption would mean that God could send us away from heaven once we got there.

RESEARCH FROM:

1. "Marriage," *The Universal Jewish Encyclopedia*, ed. Isaac Landman (New York: Universal Jewish Encyclopedia Co., Inc., 1948).
2. "Betrothal," *The Jewish Encyclopedia*, ed. Isidore Singer (New York: Funk and Wagnals Company, 1907).
3. George B. Eager, "Marriage," *The International Standard Bible Encyclopedia*, ed. James Orr (Grand Rapids: Wm. B. Eerdmans Publishing Company, 1957).
4. Emma Williams Gill, *Home Life in the Bible* (Nashville: Broadman Press, 1936).
5. James Neil, *Everyday Life in the Holy Land* (New York: Cassell and Company, Ltd., 1913).
6. J. Jeremias, *Theological Dictionary of the New Testament*, ed. Gerhard Kittel, trans. and ed. Geoffrey We. Bromiley, IV (Grand Rapids: Wm. B. Eerdmans Publishing Co., 1967).

GOD DESIGNED MARRIAGE TO ILLUSTRATE:

CHRIST'S RELATIONSHIP WITH THE CHURCH

CHRIST AND THE CHURCH	HUSBAND AND WIFE
1. Christ has made a lasting covenant with the Church.	The husband and wife are to make a lasting covenant with each other. (See Ephesians 5:31-32.)
2. Christ is the head of the Church. (See Ephesians 5:23.)	The husband is to be the head of the marriage. (See I Corinthians 11:3.)
3. The function of Christ is to care for and protect the Church. (See Matthew 16:18.)	The function of the husband is to provide for and protect his wife. (See Ephesians 5:28-30.)
4. Christ has a special ministry of purifying the Church by His Word. (See Ephesians 5:25-27.)	The husband has a special responsibility to purify his wife by the Word of God. (See Ephesians 5:28-29.)
5. Christ will never divorce the Church, even though there is adultery within the Church. (See James 4:4.)	The husband and the wife must never divorce each other, even though there is unfaithfulness in the marriage. (See Malachi 2:13-16; Hosea 2:14-20; Colossians 3:12-13; Mark 11:25-26.)

GOD DESIGNED MARRIAGE TO ILLUSTRATE:

4

THE BELIEVER'S RELATIONSHIP TO THE LAW

OUR RELATIONSHIP TO THE LAW	RELATIONSHIP TO MARRIAGE
1. We are required to keep the entire law as long as we live. (See Romans 7:1; James 2:10.)	A wife is required to obey her husband as long as he lives. (See Romans 7:2-3.)
2. When we die, we are no longer under the jurisdiction of the law. (See Romans 7:6.)	If the husband dies, the wife is no longer under his authority. (See Romans 7:3.)
3. When Christ lived, He fulfilled the law; and when He died, He overcame the power and penalty of the law. (See Romans 8:3; Matthew 5:17.)	The husband is required to find his strength in the Lord, not in himself. (See Proverbs 3:5-6.)
4. When we became Christians, we became a part of Christ's spiritual body. As such, we retroactively participated in His death, burial, and resurrection. (See Romans 10:4; Colossians 2:20.)	In order to experience all that God planned for a marriage, a husband and wife must become Christians and then enter into Christ's resurrection power in order to bring forth fruit to God. (See Romans 7:4.)

REBUILDING GOD'S DESIGN FOR MARRIAGE:

APPLYING THE PRINCIPLES OF SCRIPTURE TO THE MARRIAGE QUESTIONS OF OUR DAY

1. Why marriage standards must not change with culture

God designed marriage as a human object lesson of several divine relationships. To change marriage standards would be to alter the truth taught by the object lessons.

God warns not to add to His Word, nor to take from it. (See Revelation 22:18-19.) This includes trying to change Scripture by culture. If Scripture were intended to be adapted to culture, it would mean that culture would have more authority than the Bible; and since culture is determined by man's ideas, it would put man above God.

2. Why marriages before salvation are binding

When God established marriage, He did not restrict its laws and limitations just to Christians. It is the basic social structure for all people. The Pharisees were not Christians, yet Christ declared that they were responsible to obey God's marriage laws. John the Baptist condemned Herod for violating God's marriage laws, and it is quite obvious that Herod was not a Christian. (See Matthew 14:3-4.)

In I Corinthians 7, Scripture deals with the problem of a Christian's marriage to a non-Christian. It is assumed that the marriage took place when both were non-Christians. The Scripture teaches that every effort should be made to continue that marriage even though one partner is still unsaved. (See I Corinthians 7:12-14.)

In I Peter 3, God gives further instruction to Christian women on how to win their non-Christian husbands. Here again, God is reinforcing the validity of marriages which took place prior to salvation.

3. How the wrong person becomes the right person after marriage

It may be that you married one whom God never intended for you to marry. However, once you are married, that person becomes the right life partner. You can be certain of this fact because of God's commitment to work through whatever relationship we are in, in order to perfect the character of Christ in us. (See Philippians 2:13.) God makes it clear throughout Scripture that He is more concerned about building the character of Christ in us than in the relationships and circumstances required to do it. When His character is developed in your life, you will find it reflected in the lives of those around you. This will result in unexpected dimensions of genuine love and lasting peace. (See I Corinthians 13:7; Proverbs 16:7.)

4. How Christ restores what Adam and Eve corrupted

God established the wife's submission and the husband's leadership prior to the fall of Adam and Eve. The very purpose for which Eve was created was to be a help meet to Adam. In order for an assistant to be effective, there must be willing submission to leadership.

When Adam and Eve sinned, two things were corrupted: first, the loving leadership of the husband, and second, the willing submission of the wife. The wife now desires to control her husband, and the husband has a desire for unquestioned authority. "... Thy desire shall be to thy husband, and he shall rule over thee" (Genesis 3:16). At the same time, the wife wants her husband to be a spiritual leader to her, and the husband wants to avoid the responsibility of leadership. These opposing desires produce major conflicts in the marriage.

Christ came into the world to provide the power and the picture to restore the original marriage relationship. He illustrates to the wife how to submit to her husband by the way He willingly humbled Himself to the will of His Father. (See Philippians 2:6-8.) He teaches the husband how to love his wife by the way He laid down His life for the Church. (See Ephesians 5:25.)

5. Why the wife has more power than her husband

Most women do not realize that they have more power in the marriage than their husbands have. This is based on the fact that there are two types of power in the world: the power of position, such as the president of a country, and the power of influence, such as those who advise the president. History clearly confirms that those in positions of influence have more power than those who are in positions of authority. The wife is in the position of influence. Queen Esther is an example to the wife on how to influence a ruthless and tyrannical husband. (See the book of Esther.) Bathsheba demonstrates how to influence a feeble and aged husband. (See I Kings 1:11-31.) These and many other wives used their power of influence to direct their husbands. This power is also available to a wife whose husband is abusing her.

There is, however, one requirement that the wife must have— Godly attitudes. Very often a husband's reaction is triggered by a wife's wrong attitudes. This is emphasized by Peter when he explains how a believing wife can even win a non-believing husband without a word. (See I Peter 3:1-4.)

6. How to live with an unreasonable husband

God commands husbands to love their wives, and wives to reverence their husbands. But how can a wife reverence her husband when he demonstrates ungodly attitudes? The key involves separating the husband's ungodly attitude from his God-given position.

A policeman may have a terrible disposition. That gives no basis to disregard his instructions. When a wife separates her husband's personality from his position, she is able to reverence God's working through her husband to perfect Christ's character in her.

7. Why gratefulness is the key to a happy marriage

The importance of gratefulness cannot be overemphasized. It is the basis of happiness. An unhappy wife is a public rebuke to her husband. Her sad countenance proclaims the message, "See what a failure my husband is; he doesn't know how to meet my needs." On the other hand, a happy wife is a credit to her husband.

The basic cause of unhappiness is unfulfilled expectations. Prior to marriage, a wife usually has a list of expectations for her husband. If he fulfills the expectations, everything is fine; but if he fails to fulfill some of them, the wife becomes hurt and disappointed. In reality, this makes the husband a prisoner of his wife's expectations.

In response, the husband will tend to do all he can to reduce the number of expectations his wife has for him. He wants her to expect as little as possible so that he can go beyond her expectations and enjoy her admiration.

It is a wise wife who will give her expectations to God. By giving them to God, she frees Him to work through her husband to meet her needs. She then can say with confidence, "My soul, wait thou only upon God; for my expectation is from him" (Psalm 62:5).

Men are drawn to a grateful spirit. Equally strong is their reaction to an ungrateful or demanding spirit.

8. What really fulfills a wife

Every person finds his or her identity, not by doing what they want to do, but by discovering and fulfilling the purpose for which God made them. God made a wife to be a help meet to her husband. She will find true fulfillment in developing a servant's spirit. What is meant by a servant's spirit? It means becoming excited about making someone else successful. God will always bless this kind of an attitude. The paradox is that the more a wife serves to make her husband successful, the more freedom and authority will be given to her.

Joseph illustrated this when he served in Potiphar's house. He began as a slave, but soon was in charge of the whole household. (See Genesis 39.) Christ also illustrated this principle during His earthly ministry. "And being found in fashion as a man, he humbled himself, and became obedient unto death, even the death of the cross. Wherefore God also hath highly exalted him, and given him a name which is above every name" (Philippians 2:8-9).

9. The power of appeal with a quiet spirit

God warns that a wife who takes matters into her own hands will destroy her house. (See Proverbs 14:1.) Instead, God wants the wife to learn how to appeal wisely to her husband and to the Lord, and to learn the secret of having a quiet spirit. A quiet spirit is one that does not give way to hysterical fear or worry. (See I Peter 3:4.)

This is not to say that the wife should just let tragedies happen. She must first identify her responsibilities and perform them in God's wisdom and power; then she must follow through on careful, prayerful appeals to her husband. In cases where the law is being broken, the appeal would have to go beyond the husband if correction is not made.

The wife must recognize that God wants her to be strong in faith and to fulfill her Scriptural responsiblities through His power. The secret of her authority is not so much in her husband as it is in the Lord.

A Godly woman can trust God to change the heart of her husband. This was the secret of Sarah. Her trust was not in Abraham, but rather in the Lord. "For after this manner in the old time the holy women also, who trusted in God, adorned themselves, being in subjection unto their own husbands: Even as Sarah obeyed Abraham, calling him lord . . ." (I Peter 3:5-6).

10. Love begins with a decision, not an emotion

God has given holy standards for marriage, but these standards can only be achieved by God's power within us. If we try to keep them in our own strength, we will fail and experience guilt. At that point we have two choices: Acknowledge that God's standards are just and plead for His mercy and grace; or lower God's standards to the point that we can keep them with our own energy. This lowering of God's standards results in "fairness" theology through which "every man does that which is right in his own eyes" (paraphrase of Judges 21:25). For this reason God wants us to decide to have His power and live in Christ's victory, rather than basing marriage on the changing emotions of affection.

11. The value of marriage conflicts

There is uniform agreement that God established marriages to be life-long commitments, but there are opposing viewpoints regarding the value of marriage conflicts.

We do not like to live with irreconcilable differences in our marriages. Sooner or later we will find reasons to support our need to end the conflict. The problem is that life must be lived in anticipation of daily struggles; but God is able to turn impossible conflicts into true victory and peace when we learn the lessons He has for us and develop the character of Christ in our lives.

12. Why a "fifty-fifty" marriage does not work

God compares the Church's relationship with Christ to a wife's relationship with her husband. It is obvious that the Church is subject to Christ. It is under the authority and protection of Christ and is to be obedient to His words. At the same time, the husband is to lay down his life for his wife just as Christ laid down His life for the Church. (See Ephesians 5:22-33.)

A further problem of a "fifty-fifty" marriage is its effect upon the children. God warns that no one can serve two masters. (See Matthew 6:24.) When children can sense equal authority in their parents, they become frustrated and will carry out the further warnings of this verse: they will either hate the one and love the other or cling to one and despise the other.

13. The cause and cure of public rejection

Many divorced people sense rejection. Whether this rejection is real or imagined, it is important to understand its cause and purpose.

God has put a special reverence for marriage in the hearts of all people. Marriage is the very foundation of every civilization. If the foundation is corrupt, the civilization becomes corrupt.

To insure strong, lasting marriages, God has put a special stigma on anyone who violates the marriage vow. This stigma is referred to in Proverbs 6:30-33: "Men do not despise a thief, if he steal to satisfy his soul when he is hungry; But if he be found, he shall restore sevenfold; he shall give all the substance of his house. But whoso committeth adultery with a woman lacketh understanding: he that doeth it destroyeth his own soul. A wound and dishonour shall he get; and his reproach shall not be wiped away." This reproach will be greatly reduced as you become an effective rebuilder.

14. Why divorces break people, not marriages

A legal divorce will end the physical relationships in the marriage, but the "cleaving" aspect of a marriage pictures a much deeper union than just the physical. God states that two shall become one flesh. (See Genesis 2:24.)

The "one flesh" concept can be illustrated by joining two pieces of plywood with a strong binding glue. If you try to separate the plywood, you splinter both pieces of wood rather than dividing the glue. In that sense divorce breaks people, not marriages.

David committed adultery with Bathsheba and arranged for her husband to be killed. Then David married Bathsheba; yet God continued to call Bathsheba the wife of Uriah. (See II Samuel 12:15.)

The divorce may separate a couple physically, but the witness of their being one flesh will live on in the physical characteristics of their children.

The man in Malachi 2:13-16 divorced the wife of his youth, yet God continued to hold him responsible for his treachery to his wife. As a result, his prayers and weeping were not heard.

15. Why only death ends a marriage

One of God's basic truths of redemption is explained on the basis that marriage can only end by death. To change the marriage standard is to change the truth of God into heresy.

The truth is contained in Romans 7. We are bound to the law until our death; but once we die in Christ, we are free to be joined to Christ. If we could divorce our old master and marry Christ without death, there would have been no need for Christ to die or for us to enter into His death. (See Romans 7:1-2.)

God adds emphasis to this Scriptural truth by referring to the sinfulness of a woman's remarrying while her husband is still living. "So then if, while her husband liveth, she be married to another man, she shall be called an adulteress: but if her husband be dead, she is free from that law; so that she is no adulteress, though she be married to another man" (Romans 7:3).

16. The hidden destruction of a "happy" remarriage following a divorce

Most people are unaware of the tremendous tensions and difficulties of a second marriage. Those who judge marital happiness by outward appearance rarely know the real facts. However, let us assume that a divorced and remarried couple works through unforeseen conflicts and achieves, at least for the present, a happy marriage. Without knowing it, they have become a weakening force to many marriages. When they tell their friends how happy they are and how blessed their new marriage is, they encourage those with weak or struggling marriages to think, "Why should we continue in this unhappy marriage? If God has blessed their new marriage, He could also bless us if we divorce and remarry."

Pastors have affirmed that one of the greatest problems that they face in trying to talk people out of a divorce are other people who have already divorced and remarried and who appear to be happy in their new relationships. Because of this conflict, it is very important for divorced people to acknowledge the wrongness of their action with a repentant spirit and explain, "If you see God's blessing on my life, it is not His vindication of what I did; it is His blessing on a repentant spirit."

17. How to provide a "father image" with no father

God gives clear testimony in Scripture that even if sons and daughters do not have a father image in the family, they may still become well-adjusted and effective adults.

Timothy was one of the most effective early Church leaders, yet he did not have the influence of a father or grandfather when he was growing up. His Hebrew mother had married a Greek man. We know that this man had little regard for God's ways, since he did not follow the sacred Scriptural command to have Timothy circumcised. (See Acts 16:3.)

Timothy's mother followed some very wise steps.

- She united with her mother in rearing Timothy. (See II Timothy 1:5.)
- She taught Timothy the Scriptures so that he would understand that God was his father. (See II Timothy 3:15.)
- She strengthened her faith in what God could do for her and for Timothy. (See II Timothy 1:5.)
- She caused Timothy to admire Godly Christian leaders in the early Church. Based on this, it was quite natural for Paul to spiritually adopt Timothy as his son in the faith. (See I Timothy 1:2.)

18. How Christ established God's highest marriage standards

The Pharisees asked Jesus, "... Is it lawful for a man to put away his wife for every cause?" (Matthew 19:3). Christ's answer is significant. He did not become embroiled in a multitude of arguments which they could present from the law of Moses. He went back to God's original design for marriage. "And he answered and said unto them, Have ye not read, that he which made them at the beginning made them male and female, And said, For this cause shall a man leave father and mother, and shall cleave to his wife: and they twain shall be one flesh? Wherefore they are no more twain, but one flesh. What therefore God hath joined together, let not man put asunder" (Matthew 19:4-6).

19. Why the "exception clause" does not refer to marital unfaithfulness

The main argument of those who justify divorce and remarriage is the exception clause in Matthew 19:7-8 (also in Matthew 5:32). These verses were not in Christ's original answer to the deceptive question of the Pharisees. Had the Pharisees been sincerely wanting to do God's will, they would have accepted Christ's initial answer which reemphasized God's order in creation. God made no provision for divorce when he instituted marriage. (See Genesis 2:23-24.)

There are certain illegal marriages which are to be terminated according to Scriptural command, such as incestuous marriages and sodomite marriages.

The man in the Corinthian church who married his father's wife was condemned by Paul for his incestuous relationship. His sin is named as *porneia* (fornication) in I Corinthians 5:1. Incestuous marriages are condemned in Leviticus 18.

A marriage between two men or two women was also condemned as an illegal marriage in Leviticus 18:22. The word *ekporneuo* (fornication) is used for sodomy in Jude 7.

The law of Moses also allowed a man to put away his bride if he found that she was unfaithful between the time of their engagement and marriage.

In the time of Christ, an engaged couple was considered to be legally married. To break the engagement would, therefore, require a legal divorce. While Joseph and Mary were still engaged, but before they had phyically consummated their marriage, Mary was with child by the Holy Spirit. Because Joseph loved Mary and did not want to make her a public example, he considered quietly divorcing her. (See Matthew 1:18-20.)

Christ's exception clause in Matthew 5 and 19 certainly referred to the three cases listed above.

If we enlarge the definition of "fornication" (Greek word *porneia*) beyond these three, we would justify divorce for everyone; for who has not been guilty of some form of mental or physical immorality?

If we say that the word *fornication* means adultery in the marriage, we face a whole new set of questions, including:

- Who is the "innocent party"?
- What about our calling to suffer for righteousness?
- What about the restrictions on going to law?
- What about the "exceptions" to the "exception clause," such as Deuteronomy 22:28-29.

(See further information at the end of this chapter.)

20. What the phrase "not under bondage" really means

I Corinthians 7:13-15 deals with a Christian whose unbelieving spouse left because he or she did not want to live with a Christian. "But if the unbelieving depart, let him depart. A brother or a sister is not under bondage in such cases: but God hath called us to peace" (I Corinthians 7:15). This is not a phrase to establish remarriage. That would be contrary to the whole teaching of the chapter. It is a challenge for the believing partner to pray for spiritual peace in the unbelieving spouse.

I Corinthians 7:16 clearly explains this: "For what knowest thou, O wife, whether thou shalt save thy husband? or how knowest thou, O man, whether thou shalt save thy wife?" When a Christian has an unbelieving partner who leaves, the Christian demonstrates a lack of faith by marrying someone else. The Christian also cuts off the possiblility of God's saving the partner and re-establishing the marriage.

If an unbelieving husband divorces his wife, she is no longer bound by civil law to her husband, but she is still under God's law. (See I Corinthians 7:39; Romans 7:2.)

Thus a divorced woman is not required to obey her former husband. However, she must continue to obey the commands of God, which include honoring the Scriptural picture which marriage portrays.

The phrase "a brother or sister is not under bondage in such cases" is widely used to support remarriage after divorce or desertion. Yet the further teachings of I Corinthians 7 clearly encourage singleness, not remarriage.

21. The difficulty of an innocent party

If we accept "fairness theology" and become emotionally involved in charges and counter-charges of a marriage conflict, we will be tempted to think in terms of an innocent party and a guilty party. However, if we apply God's just standards to both husband and wife, we will quickly see that there is no innocent party. One partner may be the major contributor to the marriage dissolution at the present time, but a wider investigation will usually reveal causes and failures on the other side as well.

Can a husband claim to be the innocent party when God holds him responsible to cleanse his wife from all impurity by the Word? (See Ephesians 5:25-28.)

Can a wife claim to be following Scripture when she rejects the ministry and rewards of suffering for righteousness' sake, which God calls every Christian to accept? (See I Peter 2:18—3:10.)

The motivation to find an innocent party is usually for the purpose of justifying divorce and remarriage. God gives no Scriptural freedom for remarriage. This is clearly taught in Matthew 5:32. God states that a husband who divorces his wife and marries another commits adultery. If adultery were Scriptural grounds for remarriage, the woman whose husband divorced her and became an adulterer would certainly have grounds for remarriage. Yet God warns that anyone who marries her will also commit adultery. (See Matthew 5:32.)

22. The misleading idea that God divorced Israel

Many are using this Scriptural metaphor to reason that, if God gave a divorce to Israel, there are just grounds for a husband or wife to give their partner a divorce today. This analogy breaks down in several points.

- God's action does not give us automatic license to do the same. For example, God can bring about vengeance, but He warns us not to try it. ". . . Vengeance is mine; I will repay, saith the Lord" (Romans 12:19).

- God's dealing with Israel was not designed to cut her off permanently, but rather to bring her to repentance and restore her to Himself. According to God's promise, Israel will one day return to Him.

- To justify divorce because God gave Israel a bill of divorcement would make it possible for us to justify bigamy also, because God used the analogy of being married to both Israel and Judah.

- We can be sure that the Scripture in Jeremiah is not teaching the kind of divorce being practiced today. In Jeremiah 3:8, God administers judgment to backsliding Israel by "putting her away and giving her a bill of divorcement"; however, there is no mention of God giving a divorce to treacherous Judah. In verse 14, God concludes that He is still married to them. "Turn, O backsliding children, saith the Lord; for I am married unto you . . . ."

NEW RESEARCH ON THE "EXCEPTION CLAUSE"

A national conference was held in September 1981 to study the question of divorce and remarriage. Bible scholars from around the country were invited to come and present research papers on this subject.

During the conference, various views were given; however, clear and substantial evidence was presented by various scholars to establish the following points:

1. That there are no Scriptural grounds for divorce on the basis of adultery.
2. That the "exception clause" does *not* refer to marital unfaithfulness.
3. That the "exception clause" *does* refer to illegal marriages such as incest. It may also refer to immorality during the Jewish betrothal period.
4. That the position of the "exception clause" syntactically does not allow remarriage under any condition while the other partner is still living.
5. That this view was accepted almost unanimously by the early Church leaders, who were much closer to Christ's time and teachings than we are today.
6. That the view that divorce and remarriage are permissible for unfaithfulness in the marriage can be traced back to the 15th century humanist, Erasmus.

The research behind these conclusions came from a thorough study of Scripture and also a study of the early church fathers. Excerpts from these papers are included on the following pages.

BIBLICAL TEACHING ON DIVORCE AND REMARRIAGE

Dr. Charles C. Ryrie*

"The Mosiac law nowhere provided for divorce, though people who lived during that period practiced it. The importance of this point cannot be overstressed, especially in light of statements by evangelicals who, after discussing Deuteronomy 24:1-3, not that "God permitted divorce within stringently defined limits" (Jay Adams, *Marriage, Divorce and Remarriage in the Bible*,Phillipsburg, N. J.: Presbyterian and Reformed, 1980, p. 30). In fact the passage only recognizes that divorce was being practiced but it never prescribes it (cf. Isaksson, pp. 21, 25).

"Deuteronomy 24:1-4 has been used by evangelical Protestants to demonstrate that 'the divorce permitted or tolerated under the Mosiac economy had the effect of dissolving the marriage bond,' therefore, with reference to our Lord's teaching in Matthew 5:32 and 19:9 'we should not expect that remarriage would be regarded as adultery' (John Murray, *Divorce*, Philadelphia: Orthodox Presbyterian Church, 1953, pp. 41-42; cf. Guy Duty, *Divorce and Remarriage*, Minneapolis: Bethany, 1967, pp. 32-44). In reality this is a misuse of the passage.

"First, notice that

> ... the legislation relates only to particular cases of remarriage; the protasis contains incidental information about marriage and divorce, but it does not legislate on those matters. The verses do not institute divorce, but treat it as a practice already known ... (Peter C. Craigie, *The Book of Deuteronomy*, NICOT, Grand Rapids: Eerdmans, 1976, pp. 304-5).

"The passage acknowledges the existence of the practice of divorce; it regards the second marriage as legal: and it forbids the reinstitution of the first marriage even after the death or divorce of the second spouse. In particular it forbids the remarriage of the first spouse on the grounds that the one flesh bond with the first husband still exists, even though divorce has been effected. Thus the passage teaches *exactly the opposite* from what Murray claims. The first marriage is not 'dissolved'; otherwise, there would be no basis for prohibiting that remarriage (see G. J. Wenham, 'The Restoration of Marriage Reconsidered' [Deut. 24:1-4] *Journal of Jewish Studies* 30 [1979]: 36-40 and *Third Way* 1:21 [November 3, 1977]: 7-9).

---

*Author of *Ryrie Study Bible*.

"In summary, there appears to be three major problems with the evangelical Protestant view. First, it cannot substantiate equating *porneia* with *moicheia* (see esp. Isaksson, pp. 131-35). Second, if it could, then it would not be able to account for the disciples' reaction in Matthew 19:10. Third, the position of the exception clause in the protasis of Matthew 19:9 does not lead to the conclusion that it modifies both verbs; therefore, even if divorce is permitted, remarriage is not . . . .

"Like the Lord, Paul disallowed divorce. He did recognize that the unbelieving partner in a spiritually mixed marriage might leave (and subsequently divorce) in which case the believer could not prevent it. But in no case was the believer free to remarry, the legal facet of any marriage may be dissolved, but the one flesh relationship (and vows made to God) does not become non-existent until the death of one of the partners . . . ."

A RE-EXAMINATION OF THE DIVORCE QUESTION

Paul E. Steele*

"Dr. Gordon Wenham, Lecturer in Semetic studies at Queens University, Belfast, contends that there is never a possibility of remarriage after divorce for any cause[1] (except, of course, the death of the former spouse).[2] He does not appeal to the critical school (as some do) to remove the exception clause, nor does he deal extensively with the possible meanings of *porneia*, rather he proves (I believe conclusively) that it was Christ's intent that there be no remarriage of either party under any conditions.

"Part of his appeal is based on the reactions of the disciples in Matthew 19:10: 'His disciples say unto Him, If the case of the man be so with his wife, it is not good to marry.' Wenham's argument is clear. If Christ was only supporting the rabbinical school of Shammai (as some teach, i.e. *porneia=moicheia*) then why the astonishment?[3]

"The master stroke, however, is the opinion of the early Church fathers, a position he refers to as the 'patristic interpretation'. He points out that in the 16th century, *Erasmus* introduced the idea that has been taken over by protestant theologians. The position known as 'the traditional protestant interpretation' is best represented in John Murray's extensive work, *Divorce*.[4] It holds that the

* Pastor, Valley Church, Cupertino, California.

one exception to Christ's teaching of 'no divorce' is adultery and because of that act, dissolution of a marriage is allowed (though not preferred), and the permission to remarry the 'innocent' party is assumed . . . .

"Dr. Wenham, using a volume by a French scholar, H. Crouzel, and other sources, says: 'Great weight should be given to the fathers' interpretation of Matthew 19:9. Being closest in time to the composition of the gospels, they are most likely to have understood the original intentions of the writers. They thought and wrote in Greek with a fluency no modern scholar can match and therefore what may seem to us to be obscure may well have appeared quite plain to them. Furthermore, they are likely to have preserved memories of dominical precept and apostolic practice that guided their interpretation of the relevant N. T. passages. It is therefore intrinsically probable that the patristic interpretation of this verse is the correct one.' (Some would disagree with Wenham's confidence in the early church fathers, but it does not blunt his argument when all factors are considered).[5] 'The fathers show almost total unanimity on the question: All Greek writers and all Latin writers except one in the first five centuries agree that following divorce for any cause, remarriage is adulterous. The marriage bond unites both parties until the death of one of them.'[6]

"Dr. Wenham identifies the one dissenter as Ambrosiaster, a Latin writer of the fourth century. He allowed remarriage for the husband only and also held that remarriage was allowed for desertion. 'But', says Wenham, 'his views find no echo in the fifth century Latin writers, among whom Jerome and Augustine discuss the issues very fully.'[7]

"Dr. Wenham concedes that divorce and remarriage took place in the early church and even points out that Origen mentions that certain bishops permitted remarriage to prevent worse ills, but all recognized it was 'contrary to Scripture.'[8] Wenham says, 'The canons of various councils set out the severe discipline imposed on those who disregarded the official teaching and remarried. But all the fathers save Ambrosiaster are agreed that Christ never intended remarriage.'[9] Wenham then deals with the New Testament teaching on the subject other than Matthew, after which he gives a thorough summary of the Matthean context of Matthew 19 and then turns his attention to the major problems in Erasmus' view.

"First, Erasmus would have Christ contradicting Himself and siding with Shammai.

"Second, he did not properly understand that while divorce always assumed remarriage in Jewish culture, Christ made it clear that was not the case.

"Third, Erasmus ignored the problem with Matthew 5:32. The early church fathers interpreted that as a possible separation, but not remarriage. If Erasmus' view were held, the 'innocent' wife who is divorced by her husband could not remarry, but the unchaste wife divorced because of fornication could. Finally, the Erasmus interpretation makes verse 32a contradict 32b (whoever marries a divorced woman commits adultery).[10]

"Dr. Wenham says: 'The conflict can be simply resolved if we admit that for whatever reason a wife is put away, neither she nor her husband are free to remarry. Once again the patristic interpretation makes Matthew self-consistent, whereas the Erasmus interpretation introduces a contradiction.'[11]

"Wenham's closing paragraph summarizes it clearly.

How then does our God's teaching differ from that of the Old Testament which we considered in the previous article? In two respects he develops and deepens the Old Testament teaching on marriage and divorce. The Old Testament defined adultery as infidelity by a married woman; Jesus insisted that unfaithfulness by a married man was adultery against his wife. He thereby established full reciprocity between the sexes and implicitly excluded the possibility of polygamy. Second, the Old Testament regarded marriage as a life-long commitment, but it did permit divorce. However by restricting the freedom to remarry after divorce in certain directions, the Old Testament implies that the bond between the original couple still subsists. Jesus affirmed this explicitly. For him any remarriage after divorce is adultery against the first spouse. His disciples may therefore separate where one party is guilty of unchastity, but that does not give the other the right to remarry. He must remain faithful to his first love, even when his love is not returned, 'for the sake of the kingdom of heaven.' In so doing he will be following a divine pattern of the Lord who remained faithful to faithless Israel, of Christ who died for unworthy sinners.[12]

"Holding with Wenham that remarriage is expressly forbidden in the text, no matter what the cause, there is a third, and often forgotten, interpretation of the word *porneia*. It was within the realm of Jewish terminology and was based upon the marriage restrictions of the Old Testament law. Now keep in mind that in Matthew 19 the law is the issue. Verse 3: 'Is it lawful?' Verse 4: 'Have you not read?' Verse 7: 'Did not Moses then command . . .?' Verse 8: 'Moses . . . permitted', and the audience is primarily the scribe and Pharisee, legal experts. They are trying to trap Christ in a fine point of the law by appealing to Deuteronomy and the . . . [regulation] of Moses in regard to the marriage contract (a . . . [regulation] that was . . . [given] simply because divorce was a reality, and there had to be a protection in preference to the possibility of one man switching from one woman to another and then back to the original one).

"Now this meaning of *porneia* would be understood by the Jews to be legal terminology and not classical usage, since the context is that of a discussion of the law. What *porneia* meant in such a case was that there were marriages which were not considered valid because they were outside the prohibited Levitical decree.

"Now it is interesting to me that scholars who insist that *porneia* means 'adultery' in Matthew 19, equally insist that the same word means marriage outside the Levitical decree in a passage like Acts 15:20. For example, in the *Theological Dictionary of the New Testament*, nearly sixteen pages are given to this word. In most every case it interprets the meaning of *porneia* to be either 'general immorality' (with special emphasis on temple prostitutes) or 'adultery'; but when it comes to a discussion of the usage of this word in the book of Acts, it says:

> The only word of the group used in Acts is *porneia* and this occurs only three times in verses recording the prohibitions of the Apostolic Decree, 15:20, 29 and 21:25. In content the decree is a concession to Gentile Christians. There is no insistence on the Jewish law, only on the observance of minimal requirements for the interrelationships of Jewish and Gentile Christians—15:28. Among these is the prohibition of fornication. As is well known, some important witnesses to the western text reduce the prohibitions to three by omitting *pnikton* (strangled), and add the so-called Golden Rule, Matt. 7:12. The whole decree is thus presented, not as a ritual order, but as a short moral catechism, which mentions negatively the three chief sins (idolatry, murder, and fornication) and positively the basic ethical rule. In all probability, however, this is a secondary simplification. *The surprising combination of* porneia *with dietary regulations is due to the fact that the four prohibitations are based on Leviticus 17 and 18.* Porneia *here is marrying within the prohibited degrees, which according to the rabbis, were forbidden 'on account of fornication'—Lev. 18:6-18.* [13]

F. F. Bruce says in *The Acts of the Apostles*:

> It seems strange to find an injunction against fornication coupled with food regulations. Illicit sexual relations were, however, regarded very lightly by the Greeks, and *porneia* was closely associated with several of their religious festivals. Here the word should probably be taken in a special sense of breaches of the Jewish marriage law, Leviticus 18, which was taken over by the church. W. K. Lowther Clark, *New Testament Problems - 1929*, p. 29 finds the same meaning in Matt. 5:32; 19:9. [14]

"He then turns around and says, 'In I Cor. 6:13, etc., *porneia* is used, of course, in the widest sense.

"Now what were the marriage restrictions of Leviticus 18? Chapter 17 of Leviticus explains the relationship of the people of Israel with blood, which affected the dietary restrictions that are mentioned in Acts 15. In chapter 18 Moses gives the Word of the Lord relative to the importance of standing in contrast to the Canaanites in the land in which they lived. He gives a number of areas of unlawful sexual relationships. Thus, this was taken by the Jews (and rightly so) to be also a matter of forbidding marriage in

certain areas. Verses 6-18 deal with the subject of incest. In fact, incest, of all kinds, going far beyond the present-day understanding of incest, even including a daughter-in-law and a sister-in-law. God flatly calls it 'wickedness' (verse 17).

"Such marriages would be considered *porneia* and would therefore be null and void: A marriage outside the allowable boundaries of God's permission. Therefore, for possible genetic reasons, and as a testimony to a society which allowed unrestricted marriage, one should be given a permissible divorce. If you think this would be impossible in our day, you should read the article in *Time Magazine*, April 14, 1980, 'Attacking the Last Taboo',[15] and the article from *Psychology Today*, Mar. 1980, on 'The Pro-Incest Lobby.'[16] I would suggest you plan to be shocked. There are forces abounding today that want to break down all barriers to free sex and advocate mother-son marriages, father-daughter marriages and brother-sister marriages as permissible and 'normal.' Could it not be possible we will again face the situation of I Cor. 5:1, '. . . such fornication as is not so much as named among the Gentiles . . . . ' Thank God, courts have so far struck down attempts to recognize 'close kin marriages,' but how long can they hold out in an age that allows homosexuality to run rampant?

"If an incestuous marriage were made legal and after a time those involved became Christian, would you recognize that marriage? It is leaven.[17] It is wickedness. We are not even to eat with such a person until the tie is severed.[18] Legally, that would mean divorce. To the Church it is nullity. Should the parties remarry? I would say, 'No, for the Kingdom of God's sake.' After all, many people today serve God faithfully as single individuals and Paul says at times it is to be preferred to the married state (I Cor. 7:8, 27, 32, etc.). We hear critics tell us we are condemning people to a life of singleness. Some of God's greatest saints were single men and women. Were they condemned? Of course not. What they did was deny themselves for the Kingdom of God's sake, and to the glory of God. They were free to serve and God compensated for their singleness as He always does. We, frankly, have found a whole new dynamic for service in our church from the divorced-unmarried God has sent to us. When these people change their energies from seeking remarriage to simply seeking God's *best* for their lives they become a force to be reckoned with in the church and the world . . . ."

1. Wenham, Gordon, Dr., "The Biblical View of Marriage & Divorce, No. 1, The Cultural Background," *Third Way*, (London: Third Way); "The Biblical View of Marriage & Divorce, No. 2, Old Testament Teaching," *Third Way*, (London: Third Way, Nov. 3, 1977); 7-9; "The Biblical View of Marriage & Divorce, No. 3, New Testament Teaching," *Third Way*, (London: Third Way, Nov. 17, 1977), 7-9.

2. Romans 7:2-4

3. Wenham, op. cit., Nov. 17, 1977, p. 8.

4. Murray, John, *Divorce*, (Phila.: Presbyterian & Reformed Publ. Co., 1972).

5. Parenthesis mine [Pastor Steele's].

6. Wenham, op. cit., Nov. 17, 1977, p. 7.

7. Ibid.

8. Ibid.

9. Ibid.

10. Wenham, op. cit., Nov. 17, 1977, pp. 7-9.

11. Wenham, op. cit., Nov. 17, 1977, p. 9.

12. Ibid.

13. Friedrich, G., (ed), op. cit., pp. 592-3.

14. Bruce, F. F., *The Acts of the Apostles*, (Grand Rapids, Wm. B. Eerdmans Publ. Co., 1965), p. 300.

15. Anon., "Attacking the Last Taboo," *Time*, (New York: John Meyers Publ. Co., April 14, 1980), p. 72.

16. DeMott, Benjamin, "The Pro-Incest Lobby," *Psychology Today*, (New York: Ziff-Davis Publ. Co., March 1980), pp. 11-16.

17. I Corinthians 5:6-7.

18. I Corinthians 5:9-11.

Answers to Quiz 2

1. False   Marriage begins with the vow. (See Malachi 2:14.) A physical relationship does not constitute marriage. (See Deuteronomy 22:28-29; Exodus 22:16-17.)

2. False   Adultery does not free the other partner to end the marriage.

3. False   Desertion is not grounds for Scriptural divorce.

4. False   Divorce does not carry with it the right to remarry.

5. False   If one partner remarries, the other is not free to remarry.

6. False   Steps should be taken to stop divorce and those who bring it about. "What God therefore hath joined together let no man put asunder" (Matthew 19:6). A marriage should continue with or without love.

7. False   Marriages are built on the committment of a vow, not on the emotions of affection.

8. False   Every Christian is to forgive and accept a repentant adulterer, but the stigma will continue as a reminder to them and as a warning to others.

9. False   The marriage bed can be defiled by perverting God's moral standards. (See Hebrews 13:4.)

10. False   Parents who have equal authority will cause tension in the marriage and reaction from the children.

11. False   The husband should seek counsel from his wife prior to important decisions.

Personal Commitment and Accountability

In rebuilding God's design for marriage:

I am committed to the truth that God designed marriage . . .

☐ 1. To be a lifelong relationship.

This means that I do not accept any justification to get out of my marriage.

☐ 2. To be an unbreakable vow "until death do us part."

This means that if my marriage fails, I will work to be reconciled or to remain single as long as my partner is living.

☐ 3. To be a human object lesson of several divine relationships.

This means that my marriage must be consisent with the truths God is trying to teach in these relationships.

☐ 4. To be a foundation for strong churches and nations.

This means that any ministry I have to strengthen the church must include strengthening the family.

☐ 5. To be a "classroom" to learn Godly character.

This means that when my ways please the Lord, He will cause my partner to be at peace with me.

☐ 6. To be the basis of raising up Godly generations.

This means that my personal happiness and physical fulfillment are secondary to the needs of my children.

☐ 7. To be the only right way to have a physical relationship.

This means that I will not look lustfully at any other person, or visualize any other relationship.

☐ 8. To be an equal exchange of personal rights.

This means that I do not think in terms of money, my time, schedule, or body.

☐ 9. To be an example of Christ's love for the Church.

This means that I continue to love my wife and sacrifice myself for her even when she rejects me and sins against me.

☐ 10. To be an example of the Church's submission to Christ.

This means that I submit to my husband in every area except violating God's Word.

☐ 11. To be a safeguard against wrong decisions.

This means that before making any major decision, I get counsel from my partner.

☐ 12. To be above the changeable fads of culture.

This means that the principles of marriage and the family do not change when conditions change in a society.

Signed_____

Witness_____ Date_____

GOAL NUMBER **3**

REBUILDING A CLEAR CONSCIENCE AND A FORGIVING SPIRIT

"Holding faith, and a good conscience; which some having put away concerning faith have made shipwreck."

I Timothy 1:19

"But if ye forgive not men their trespasses, neither will your Father forgive your trespasses."

Matthew 6:15

Yes	No	
☐	☐	1. Is the approval of both sets of parents essential for a successful marriage?
☐	☐	2. Will conflict with parents before marriage automatically result in conflicts with your partner after marriage?
☐	☐	3. Does looking at sensual magazines, books, or films damage the marriage relationship?
☐	☐	4. If a man's wife were unfaithful to him, did the law in Deuteronomy 24:1-4 permit him to divorce her?
☐	☐	5. Do premarital relationships increase compatibility after marriage?
☐	☐	6. In the Bible, did God bring swifter punishment to immorality than to pride?
☐	☐	7. Does a divorce always bring lasting damages to the children?
☐	☐	8. Does God ever give Scriptural justification to go to a divorce court?
☐	☐	9. Can books which justify divorce and remarriage remove guilt?
☐	☐	10. Does a second marriage usually have more harmony than the first marriage?
☐	☐	11. Should secret unfaithfulness be confessed to the marriage partner?
☐	☐	12. Does asking forgiveness restore the marriage relationship?

13. Does a bitter person usually know that
he or she is bitter?

14. Does persistent bitterness mean that I am
partially guilty?

15. When a person hates his partner, does that prove
he or she hates God?

16. Can you purpose not to become like the one you
are bitter toward?

17. Can you listen to an evil report without becoming
defiled by it?

18. Does God ever prompt your marriage partner to
react to you?

19. Is it possible to be free from the temptation
of discontentment?

20. Does God expect marriage to be a struggle?

21. Can you develop a loving spirit toward your
offender by fully forgiving him?

22. Is it possible to hide bitterness?

23. Is it ever Scripturally right to be bitter?

24. Does forgiving a person also free that person
from the consequences of his or her actions?

See answers on pages 104-106.

THE PROBLEM OF GUILT BEGINS . . .

. . . Whenever we violate the principles of God's moral law. Others may assure us that we are right, but our spirits will always confirm the truth of Scripture.

A divorced woman said, "I was counseled by three pastors and my doctor to divorce my husband. I also read several books on divorce and remarriage. Each one assured me that I had Scriptural grounds for divorce. Do you think I was right in divorcing my husband?"

QUESTION:

Why are books which justify divorce and remarriage ineffective in removing guilt?

ANSWER:

Because these books appeal to the mind, but guilt is a function of the spirit. Human reasoning may convince our minds, but the conscience of our spirits still condemns us.

If this woman had three pastors and several books assure her that she was right, why did she still have a question? She was unsure of her actions because her mind told her that she was right, but her spirit told her that she was wrong.

EVIDENCES OF GUILT

EVIDENCES	EXPLANATIONS
1. DEFENSIVENESS	Guilt motivates a person to learn as many arguments as possible, because he expects a reaction to his behavior and is quick to justify what he has done. (See Proverbs 21:2.)
2. REJECTION	One who is violating God's marriage standards will sense rejection from others and will project rejection onto those who disagree with him. (See Proverbs 15:12.)
3. JUDGING	One who is guilty will usually try to offset his own guilt by pointing out similar weaknesses of others in a condemning attitude. (See Romans 2:1-3.)
4. COMPENSATION	To earn and maintain the respect of others, a guilty person will often increase his public service to God. (See I Samuel 15:22.)
5. COMPROMISE	A decision to do evil in one area will usually affect other areas as well. Standards which were formerly held high are soon rejected as being too strict. (See Proverbs 14:14.)
6. DEPRESSION	Guilt drains us of emotional energy. This soon produces emotional depression. (See Psalm 32:1-4.)
7. BREAKDOWNS	Mental and emotional breakdowns often result from the guilt of violating God's moral laws. Rejecting God's truth results in instability. (See James 1:8.)
8. ANGER	Guilt often produces a short temper and impatience with others. Frustration with one's own failures is taken out on others. (See Proverbs 12:16.)
9. FEAR	Guilt produces many fears, such as the fear of being found out and the fear of God's judgment. (See Proverbs 10:24.)

THE CAUSES OF GUILT | 2

1. Sins of your youth

Marriage does not create problems as much as it reveals problems that were never solved before marriage.

A strong will or reaction against your parents before marriage will produce a spirit of pride and independence in your marriage. This will cause your partner to react to you. Even "... God resisteth the proud ..." (James 4:6).

Immoral thoughts and actions will distort your view of marriage and cause your partner to resent you for acting out of lust rather than genuine love.

Ambitions to be rich and a focus on temporal things will destroy your ability to establish right priorities in your marriage. You will tend to sacrifice your family's interest for monetary gains.

RESPONSE TO GOD

"Remember not the sins of my youth, nor my transgressions: according to thy mercy remember thou me for thy goodness' sake, O Lord" (Psalm 25:7).

RESPONSE TO YOUR PARTNER

"God is allowing me to see how my failures in my youth have damaged my ability to make our marriage what God intended it to be. Would you forgive me?"

2. Premarital relations

Any immoral actions during one's courtship or engagement will result in devastating pressures within the marriage. If you caused or allowed your partner to violate your moral standards before marriage, you sowed the seeds of guilt, fear, mistrust, jealousy, depression, frustration, disillusionment, and self-rejection. Until this violation is specifically confessed to the Lord and then to one's spouse, there can be no forgiveness or basis for healing.

RESPONSE TO GOD

"Create in me a clean heart, O God; and renew a right spirit within me" (Psalm 51:10).

RESPONSE TO PARTNER

"I realize that I have had a wrong focus in our marital relationship. Would you forgive me of this and work with me to change my focus from getting to giving?"

3. Marriage against parents' wishes

Failure to honor the wishes of your father or mother regarding your marriage will bring God's discipline. If either your parents or your parents-in-law were against your marriage or the timing of your marriage, then God promises that things will not go well for you. God's first commandment with a promise is, "Honour thy father and thy mother . . . That it may be well with thee . . ." (Ephesians 6:1-3).

RESPONSE TO GOD

"Forgive me, O Lord, for I have not heard the instruction of my father, and I have forsaken the law of my mother" (Personalization of Proverbs 1:8).

RESPONSE TO DISAPPROVING PARENTS

"I was wrong for marrying against your wishes. I realize that I have brought great sadness to you because of what I have done. Would you forgive me?"

4. Wrong attitudes in marriage

Wrong attitudes destroy affections more quickly than wrong actions do. Anger, pride, selfishness, impatience, lust, greed, laziness, disrespect, and ungratefulness all take their toll on a marriage. They cause a partner to find acceptance and understanding outside of the marriage.

Marriage is God's most important classroom in developing Godly attitudes. When you withdraw your spirit from your partner or react when corrected, you effectively cut off vital character building.

RESPONSE TO GOD

"O Lord, produce the fruit of Your Spirit in my life: love, joy, peace, patience, gentleness, goodness, faith, meekness, self-control" (Personalization of Galatians 5:22-23).

RESPONSE TO PARTNER

"Would you forgive me for my failure to demonstrate Godly character and for not giving you the love I owe you?"

5. Inadequate preparation before marriage

Marriage is a serious responsibility. A man or woman who loves the Lord and cares deeply for the person whom he or she intends to marry will take whatever time and effort are necessary in order to be prepared for marriage.

People who rush into marriage often justify their actions with such statements as, "If we waited until we were perfect, we would never get married" or, "There are many lessons about marriage that you can only learn by being married."

RESPONSE TO GOD

"O God, forgive me for treating lightly what is sacred to You."

RESPONSE TO PARTNER

"I realize I have put great pressure on you because of my lack of preparation for marriage. I have purposed to begin concentrating on my responsibilities before God."

6. Words that damage and defile

"... The tongue is a fire, and a world of iniquity ... it defileth the whole body, and setteth on fire the course of nature; and it is set on fire of hell" (James 3:6).

Words that cut down your partner are remembered; they are like cancer in a body. Words that you use to give others a negative impression of your partner are even worse. These offending words must be dealt with as quickly as possible. Frequent checks must be made with your partner to see which words have been misunderstood or offensive to them.

RESPONSE TO GOD

"Let the words of my mouth, and the meditation of my heart, be acceptable in thy sight, O Lord, my strength and my redeemer" (Psalm 19:14).

RESPONSE TO PARTNER

"I realize the words I said to you were unkind and unloving. Would you forgive me?"

If you are divorced or separated, do not even whisper any blame or accusation against your former partner. Expect that every word you say will get back to that partner—amplified and even distorted. Rather than verbally attacking the one to whom you were married, you can use this same "grapevine" system to express praise and gratefulness to your former partner, even if he or she refuses to talk to you.

HOW TO BE FREE OF GUILT

1. Humble yourself in genuine repentance

"Be afflicted, and mourn, and weep:
let your laughter be turned to mourning,
and your joy to heaviness. Humble yourselves in the
sight of the Lord, and he shall lift you up."
James 4:9-10

REPENTANCE IS NOT	REPENTANCE IS
1. Being sorry that you failed in your marriage.	Confessing that you are proud, and then grieving over this condition of heart: "Only by pride cometh contention . . ." (Proverbs 13:10).
2. Being sorry that others have rejected you.	Confessing and grieving over the fact that you have resisted the grace which God gave you to do His will. "For it is God which worketh in you both to will and to do of his good pleasure" (Philippians 2:13).
3. Being sorry that your reputation has been damaged.	Confessing and grieving that your actions have caused God's name to be blasphemed by His enemies. (See II Samuel 12:14 and Titus 2:5.)
4. Being sorry that you lost your money or possessions.	Confessing that you have been trying to take charge of your life and that you have been following your own lusts and desires. "From whence come wars and fightings among you? come they not hence, even of your lusts that war in your members" (James 4:1).

| 5. Being sorry that you hurt your children or your partner. | Confessing that you have caused your children and your partner, for whom Christ died, to stumble by your example. (See Romans 14:13.) |
| 6. Being sorry that your plans are destroyed. | Confessing that you have had the wrong goals and priorities in life. "But seek ye first the kingdom of God, and his righteousness . . ." (Matthew 6:33). |

2. Identify your basic offense

The basic offenses involve wrong attitudes as well as wrong actions.

- ☐ Having a strong will against your parents while you were growing up.
- ☐ Becoming involved with sensual magazines, books, films, and television programs. Engaging in immoral thoughts or actions as you were growing up.
- ☐ Pursuing wrong priorities in your life. Leaving loved ones out of your schedule.
- ☐ Engaging in premarital sexual relationships.
- ☐ Getting married against the wishes of your parents or parents-in-law.
- ☐ Expressing prideful, selfish attitudes in your marriage.
- ☐ Being ungrateful and taking loved ones for granted.
- ☐ Entering into marriage without proper preparation.
- ☐ Speaking harsh, angry words. Not showing gentleness and understanding.
- ☐ Demanding your own way.
- ☐ Criticizing and belittling others. Never giving praise.
- ☐ Being deceptive and dishonest.

3. Relive your offenses through the feelings of those whom you have hurt

- True repentant attitudes come as we "feel" our offenses through the eyes and emotions of those whom we have offended.

- If we truly want forgiveness from others, we must communicate through our spirits that we understand how deeply we have hurt them.

- Those who are closest to you will often find it hard to fully forgive you until they see that you understand how deeply you hurt them. They also want to see that you have really changed, both in your attitudes and actions.

4. Think through the right wording

- Right wording will grow out of right motives and right attitudes. If your attitude is one of blame or personal irritation, your efforts will surely fail.

- Right wording will draw attention *only* to your offenses, *not* your partner's offense.

- Do not expect or demand forgiveness. Have a spirit of pleading for mercy.

- Realize that your offenses will seem much greater to the one whom you offended than they will to you. A splinter in your partner's eye against you is just a small item from your perspective, but from your partner's viewpoint, it is a beam!

- Your words should be brief, precise, and deeply sincere. (See illustration in Luke 15:11-32.)

EXAMPLE:

"God has convicted me of how wrong I have been in (precisely identify your offense). I do not deserve your forgiveness, but would you be able to forgive me for what I have done against you?"

5. Ask forgiveness of each one whom you have offended.

- The primary purpose in asking forgiveness is not to restore your marriage, but to obey God and make your ways pleasing to Him.

- Asking forgiveness does not automatically restore the broken relationship. It simply clears away the hindrances of the past so that a new relationship can be built.

- The circle of asking forgiveness should be as large as the circle of offense. Each person who has been offended should be *verbally* asked for his or her forgiveness.

- The value of a verbal request is that it allows you to be sure you are forgiven, and it allows the offender to become free of bitterness or blame toward you.

☐ ASK GOD TO FORGIVE YOU

"Have mercy upon me, O God, according to thy lovingkindness: according unto the multitude of thy tender mercies blot out my transgressions . . . . Against thee, thee only, have I sinned, and done this evil in thy sight . . ." (Psalm 51:1, 4).

☐ ASK FORGIVENESS OF YOUR PARTNER

Emphasize that you are not asking forgiveness just to restore the marriage (though you would like it restored), but to obey God and to be the person that God wants you to be, regardless of what happens in the marriage.

As you ask forgiveness, demonstrate humility and sensitivity. Do not justify yourself, and avoid any hint of blaming your partner. Explain how deeply your offenses must have hurt your partner.

☐ ASK FORGIVENESS OF YOUR PARENTS-IN-LAW

Any offense by you toward your partner will be felt deeply by his or her parents. Usually, they take up offenses against you, thereby hindering a possible restoration of the marriage.

☐ ASK FORGIVENESS OF YOUR CHILDREN

The hurts and scars in your children run very deep when you fail in your marriage. Acknowledge pride, wrong priorities, insensitivity, impatience, lack of spiritual leadership, and failure to meet their real needs.

6. Express gratitude for forgiveness

- Follow up any forgiveness with a sincere expression of gratitude. Demonstrate a change in your attitudes and actions.

- Expect time to heal the wounds of deep hurts. During this time fulfill all your responsibilities toward that person. "A brother offended is harder to be won than a strong city..." (Proverbs 18:19).

HOW A HUSBAND REMOVED GUILT
AND REBUILT A "HOPELESS" MARRIAGE

If anyone could have rebuilt a marriage, he should have been the one. He was so well-liked at college that students wildly cheered for him whenever he would walk out on the platform. But whatever he tried only caused his wife to resent him deeper. Then he followed these six steps.

For some background . . .

"I was always involved in outside activities to the neglect of my family. It seemed every sport that came around I was active and participating in it.

"My wife said that I was the most critical, insensitive, demanding, prideful person there could be; but now she says I am one of the most sensititve and loving men she has ever met.

"God had to take me through six difficult lessons to bring me to this point.

"It all came to a head one Fourth of July when we were both at home watching a ball game. I was feeling a little guilty about not being the husband I should, so I tried to gain some points by saying to my wife, 'You sure are a good wife!'

"She immediately answered, 'No, I'm not. In fact, I think we should separate. We are no longer a couple.'

"As my wife talked, there was no sign of hatred or bitterness; we had passed through that stage. Now there was just a sense of not caring.

"I decided to apply what I had learned in college, which only finalized the total separation of our marriage. Then, without hope I began learning the following lessons:

1. I finally humbled myself . . .

"Being embarrassed and deeply depressed over my failure, I stayed in the apartment and contemplated suicide. I would hear reports of what she was doing and about the other fellows she was dating and for a whole month I was unable to complete an entire meal without getting sick. I lost twenty-eight pounds. The emotional shock was so great I also broke out in boils and shingles. Not knowing what to do, I began asking advice from my friends. Their advice was to find someone else. Then one day a Seminar alumnus talked with me, and it was his advice that I followed.

"The alumnus explained to me about the spirit of a woman and how men can deeply wound this spirit. With painful humiliation, I realized that I had done everything that this alumnus had said. I felt totally responsible for my wife's actions. This broke my pride and so thoroughly humbled me that I was willing to do anything to rebuild my marriage.

"The first change that God wanted to bring to my life He accomplished by allowing a change in ownership of the apartment I was renting. I was evicted from the apartment, and I found myself at home with my parents—right where God wanted me.

2. I thanked God for allowing my wife to leave me . . .

"Admitting to God how wrong I was and gratefully accepting His forgiveness, I then sought the forgiveness of my parents, wife, and daughter. Having a clear conscience, I began asking, 'What does God want to teach me through this? Why didn't I learn this important lesson earlier in life?' God had to do all this to teach me genuine love. I thanked Him for allowing her to leave me and for giving me this opportunity to learn and show genuine love.

3. I purposed to learn what genuine love was . . .

"How could I show genuine love to the wife I had so deeply hurt? First, I tried calling her, but she didn't want to talk to me. Then I started sending her flowers. From time to time I tried to check with her to see if there was anything she needed, occasionally asking her and our daughter out for dinner. To my surprise, one day she accepted but quickly questioned my real motives. I told her, 'I want to do these things for you, and I don't ever expect anything in return. What I did to you was so wrong I don't blame you for not asking me back.' Under my breath I would add, 'All I can hope for is God's mercy because I caused one of His little ones to go astray.'

"As I was learning ways of showing genuine love, an idea came that was to be one of the hardest tests, yet it was a necessary step. Braced for ridicule, I nervously called my wife. 'Would you allow me to baby-sit while you go out Friday night on your date?' She agreed. Several days after her date, the hardest part was to come. I had purposed to ask her the following question: 'What are the character qualities that you see and appreciate in this fellow you are dating, but you never saw in my life? I would like to begin working on them, not to get you back, but to be the man God intended for me to be all along.'

4. I rebuilt communication with her parents . . .

"Through all my efforts to express genuine love, my wife continued considering the possibility of divorce. She was fully supported by her mother, who warned her to be suspicious of my new actions. Unaware of my mother-in-law's animosity toward me, God convicted me of how I had wronged her. I called, asking forgiveness for being such a poor example of a son-in-law and for the hurt I had brought to her daughter and to her. Shocked by my call, she did forgive me, and from that day on she began encouraging her daughter to see me.

5. *I began learning how to bridle my tongue . . .*

"My words were focused on my gain and rarely did I consider my wife's feelings. What could I do to break this lifelong habit? It was then that another Seminar alumnus shared with me a 'foolproof' project. He challenged me to count to fifty before answering any questions. When my wife asked a question, I acknowledged that I heard her and waited for a count of fifty, asking myself, 'Will what I'm about to say benefit her or me?' Occasionally during this period my wife was able to answer her own questions without my saying a word. Then she would thank me for my answer. 'Even a fool is counted wise when he keeps his mouth shut.'

"In learning to give genuine love, the desire to totally rebuild my marriage grew stronger and stronger. I found myself struggling and questioning my motives. One day I finally fell on my face before the Lord and cried to Him saying, 'Lord, all I want is Your mercy. Again, I give You my right to have her back. I look forward to serving You, even if it means remaining single the rest of my life.'

6. *I learned how to apply self-discipline in marriage . . .*

"Soon after I made this deeper commitment to the Lord, my wife called me. She asked if I would move back in with her solely for economic reasons; however, she made one specific stipulation. I agreed to that stipulation and moved back in with her. I was not given the right to touch her in any way. The forced discipline during this time carried over to having a consistent and rich time of prayer and reading His Word.

"It took many months before my wife believed the change in me was real, Even though she now says I am one of the most sensitive men she knows, I still say and do things that hurt her. The key is that I am now aware when that wall goes up and I can ask her forgiveness and we take care of it right away."

Used by permission

HOW A WIFE REMOVED GUILT AND
RESTORED JOY TO A DAMAGED MARRIAGE

Everyone thought we were the perfect couple, but on the inside we both had deep problems. My main problem was that I never respected my husband.

"My husband was a terrific minister of the Word of God. He has great ability to preach. He was a strong spiritual leader—but not at home. As a result, I was pulled and tugged and fretted, trying to keep our home life on an even keel.

"Because of this, I strongly admired other men who had the ability to really lead their families. I found myself wanting to be around them. Occasionally, I would mention to my husband how they did things—hoping he would get the message. He noticed but reacted. He claimed he 'was who he was' and didn't want to change.

"I was not happy, but I thought that this was my lot in life. I decided to suffer it out. Meanwhile, I began living in a fantasy world—wondering what it would be like to live with a real man.

"When we started the new church, it became necessary for both my husband and me to get outside work. I began teaching full-time but had to go back to school to pick up more courses in order to continue teaching. That's where the real trouble started.

"I met a man, my teacher. I really respected him. He was forceful, yet gentle. I just could not be around him enough. I went to classes early, stayed later—until the inevitable happened—we fell in love.

"As it turned out, he also had trouble in his marriage. We found shelter in each other. We both knew it was wrong and we tried several times to break it off. We would go sometimes a month without seeing each other, but we needed someone to talk to.

"After about a year, he kissed me one night. Up until that time it was all talk. Thank God it never went beyond that, but my guilt was so strong, I thought many times of killing myself to rid my husband of the heartache that he might have to face. I felt that I was completely beyond hope.

"I didn't expect God to let me live. I thought I'd have a car accident or some incurable disease. I knew God loved my husband too much to let him endure this heartache.

"All this time, everything was going along as usual at home—I thought. Later I found out that my husband had detected my distance and had been praying every morning at 5:00 for God to heal our marriage.

"We heard about the Basic Youth Seminar from an alumnus.

He insisted that we go. He thought it would help our ministry. We said 'O.K.' but just let it pass. We thought it was just another meeting. We had been to so many already. But this alumnus was insistent, so insistent he paid our way.

"The first night, my husband went by himself. I went to school. But when I got home that night he told me to skip school, that I needed to go. He shared some of the things in the Seminar. It sounded interesting so I decided to go also.

"That night you talked about concupiscence. I saw hope for my life. I also saw that if my husband really believed the Word of God, he would accept my mistakes and look at them as God's way of teaching both of us.

"I went home that night and confessed everything to my husband. I told him how wrong I was and I asked him to forgive me. He accepted me and said that he loved me even more, but I could tell that he was really hurt. Then I wished that I had never told him. But the next day brought new light.

"The next day you explained the principle of God's 'umbrella of protection.' When my husband saw God's great plan of responsibility for the husband, he saw himself as a possible cause for our past misery. His hurt disappeared and he asked me to forgive him for not being the man he should have been.

"It was as if we had just gotten married. We were starting over and every day was joy. We were not perfect overnight and we are still learning every day. But we are happier and our children are happier than ever before. We have made mistakes and I guess we always will, but we have a brand new hope—we see life as a stepping stone to new heights, and we know that with each mistake God will use this to make us better people."

Used by permission

EVIDENCES OF BITTERNESS

THE PROBLEM OF BITTERNESS BEGINS . . .

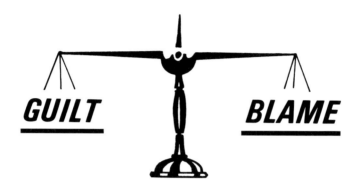

. . . When we try to balance guilt with blame. A further problem with bitterness is that those who have it often are not aware of it. They adjust to it and explain it away as hurt or disapppointment.

EVIDENCE	EXPLANATIONS
1. DEPRESSION	Guilt and bitterness burn up emotional energy. When this energy is exhausted, emotional depression results. (See Proverbs 14:10.)
2. DISTRUST	A bitter person will be very cautious of trusting others because of being hurt by people in the past. (See Hebrews 12:15.)
3. INSENSITIVITY	Bitterness causes a person to be hypersensitive to his own emotions, but insensitive to the feelings of others. A bitter person hurts others by the way he accuses them of hurting him. (See Matthew 7:2.)

4. INGRATITUDE	A bitter person expects to be compensated for the hurts that he has suffered. He feels that life and others owe him something. (See II Timothy 3:2.)
5. TENSION	Bitterness causes muscles to become tense. The muscle tone in the face becomes hard. The jaws close up tighter and put damaging pressure on the teeth. (See Acts 7:51.)
6. FLATTERY	Bitterness or resentment toward a person may be covered over by flattering lips. (See Proverbs 28:23.)
7. SICKNESS	Bitterness produces chemical imbalance. Resentment calls forth excessive hormones from the pituitary, adrenal, thyroid, and other glands. Diseases in various parts of the body result. (See Psalm 32:3-5.)
8. BONE PROBLEMS	Bitterness has a direct and devastating affect upon our bones. The marrow of our bones produces blood. Therefore, the health of our body is determined by the health of our bones, since the life of our flesh is in the blood. (See Leviticus 17:11; Proverbs 14:30; 17:22; 12:4.)
9. SELF-REJECTION	When a bitter person vows that he will never be like the one he resents, laws which produce the very opposite result go into effect. Eventually the same rejection he has toward another he also has toward himself, for he does the same things. (See Romans 2:1-3.)

5   THE CAUSES OF BITTERNESS

1. Mixing guilt with blame

It is quite natural for a marriage partner to balance his or her guilt with blame toward the other partner. For example, a husband might say, "I know that I have neglected my wife and flirted with other women, but I am bitter toward my wife for being unfaithful to me." As long as he mixes his guilt with blame, he will never conquer bitterness!

2. Attempting to get revenge

Any actions or attitudes which are designed to "teach your partner (or former partner) a lesson" will certainly fan the flames of bitterness.

3. Having temporal values

Bitterness is a reliable witness that our affections are set on the things of this world rather than on things above. (See Colossians 3:2.) The very basis of bitterness is a reaction to the loss of something temporal such as money, personal reputation, possessions, physical relationships, or future dreams.

4. Taking up offenses

When we hear an evil report about another person, it is almost impossible not to take up an offense against that person. Bitterness results, and close friendships are destroyed. ". . . A whisperer separateth chief friends" (Proverbs 16:28). "The words of a talebearer are as wounds, and they go down into the innermost parts of the belly" (Proverbs 26:22). This bitterness is not easily overcome, because we are not the recipients of the grace God gives to the offended or the offender.

STEPS TO OVERCOME BITTERNESS

6

1. Remove all guilt first

> "... First cast out the beam out of thine own eye;
> and then shalt thou see clearly to cast out the
> mote out of thy brother's eye."
>
> Matthew 7:5

Before bitterness can be conquered, we must remove all personal guilt. Any remaining guilt will prompt you to balance the guilt with bitterness and hinder you from effectively removing either one.

2. See "God's hand" through your offender

If you think that your offender is acting independently, that is, apart from any influence from God, you will never overcome bitterness.

In reality, God is working through the offense which He lovingly allows to come into your life. God's Word assures us that "Surely the wrath of man shall praise thee [God]: the remainder of wrath shalt thou [God] restrain" (Psalm 76:10).

Christ certainly illustrated this concept at His crucifixion when He said, "... Father, forgive them; for they know not what they do ..." (Luke 23:34). The further implication is clear: "But You know what You are accomplishing through them."

When David was cursed by a wicked man, David's response was "... Let him alone, and let him curse; for the Lord hath bidden him" (II Samuel 16:11).

3. Thank God for the offenses

At first, you may resist the idea of thanking God for the offenses of your partner or other members in your family. You may even feel that it is hypocritical to thank God for something for which you are not really thankful.

However, we *can* thank God without being thankful. Thanking God is an initial act of obedience by our wills. Being thankful is an expression of our emotions. Thankfulness comes as we see God's purposes through the offenses which He allows to come into our lives.

We will usually not recognize these character benefits which come from offenses until we first obey the command: "In every thing give thanks: for this is the will of God in Christ Jesus concerning you" (I Thessalonians 5:18).

4. Ask God to forgive you for temporal values and a lack of genuine love

If we are bitter, we reveal that we have set our affections on the things of this world rather than on things above. This is true, because the things that cause bitterness are temporal, not eternal.

Bitterness also proves that we lack genuine love toward the one who offended us. The Apostle Paul emphasizes this point to anyone who would go to a court of law against a brother (or marriage partner): "Now therefore there is utterly a fault among you, because ye go to law one with another. Why do ye not rather take wrong? Why do ye not rather suffer yourselves to be defrauded? Nay, ye do wrong, and defraud, and that your brethren [or marriage partner]" (I Corinthians 6:7-8).

5. Fully forgive your offender

To fully forgive your partner is to release him or her from all the broken promises, all the expectations which you had, and all of the consequences of the hurts and losses which your partner has caused you.

The only effective basis upon which we can forgive an offender is Christ's forgiveness of us: ". . . Forgiving one another, even as God for Christ's sake hath forgiven you" (Ephesians 4:32).

God waits for a sincere prayer:

"Heavenly Father, I do now fully forgive those who have offended me. I release them and ask you to release me from my bitterness."

Signed _____ Date _____

6. Restore love by voluntarily investing a "treasure" in your offender's life

Forgiving your offender does not go far enough in overcoming bitterness. Jesus taught this in Matthew 5:40–41: "And if any man will sue thee at the law, and take away thy coat, let him have thy cloak also. And whosoever shall compel thee to go a mile, go with him twain."

The principle here is very clear: God wants us to give more than is required to our offenders. He wants it to be a voluntary giving, and the result will be a new sense of love because of another principle which Jesus taught: "For where your treasure is, there will your heart be also" (Matthew 6:21).

A LIVING ILLUSTRATION

A certain man was bitter toward his former wife. She had distorted and magnified the reports of his failures in their marriage, thereby greatly damaging his reputation.

The court awarded her half of their property and assessed him monthly payments for her support. Every time he made a payment, he experienced bitterness and resentment toward her.

This man followed the steps of asking forgiveness of his wife and fully forgiving her. These steps produced a great improvement in their relationship. However, he was still lacking in love for her, and he failed to have any real joy in his Christian life. Every time he made his required payment to her, he had to fight off deep feelings of resentment. Often he thought of other ways in which he could use the money.

One day he learned the reason for his lack of joy and his failure to gain complete freedom over bitterness. He learned that he would never completely conquer bitterness until the payments that he made to his former wife were more than the required amount.

He started doing this, and to his amazement he discovered a new love for his wife, as well as a new freedom from any bitterness. The love was the result of voluntarily investing his treasure where his heart was supposed to be. The court-assigned payment was not voluntary. The overpayment was.

TYPES OF "TREASURES" YOU CAN INVEST IN THE LIVES OF YOUR OFFENDERS

☐ Investing time in praying for them.

☐ Investing words to encourage them.

☐ Investing thoughts on how they have benefited your life.

☐ Investing effort to meet a need they have.

☐ Investing trust by correcting false reports about them.

☐ Investing acceptance by showing interest in their welfare.

☐ Investing a gift to meet a basic need which they have.

1. List those who have offended you

OFFENDERS	HOW THEY OFFENDED ME

2. Identify God's purposes in each offense

OFFENSE	HOW GOD WANTS TO USE THIS OFFENSE TO CLEANSE MY LIFE AND BUILD CHARACTER

3. Recall the failures for which God should judge you

- ☐ Ungratefulness
- ☐ Strong will
- ☐ Getting angry
- ☐ Speaking harshly
- ☐ Criticizing
- ☐ Lying and deceiving
- ☐ Disobeying
- ☐ _____
- ☐ _____

4. Fully forgive your offenders

23. "Therefore is the kingdom of heaven likened unto a certain king, which would take account of his servants.

24. And when he had begun to reckon, one was brought unto him, which owed him ten thousand talents.

25. But forasmuch as he had not to pay, his lord commanded him to be sold, and his wife, and children, and all that he had, and payment to be made.

26. The servant therefore fell down, and worshipped him, saying, Lord, have patience with me, and I will pay thee all.

27. Then the lord of that servant was moved with compassion, and loosed him, and forgave him the debt.

28. But the same servant went out, and found one of his fellow-servants, which owed him an hundred pence: and he laid hands on him, and took him by the throat, saying, Pay me that thou owest.

29. And his fellow-servant fell down at his feet, and besought him, saying, Have patience with me, and I will pay thee all.

30. And he would not: but went and cast him into prison, till he should pay the debt.

31. So when his fellow-servants saw what was done, they were very sorry, and came and told unto their lord all that was done.

32. Then his lord, after that he had called him, said unto him, O thou wicked servant, I forgave thee all that debt, because thou desiredst me:

33. Shouldest not thou also have had compassion on thy fellow-servant, even as I had pity on thee?

34. And his lord was wroth, and delivered him to the tormentors, till he should pay all that was due unto him.

35. So likewise shall my heavenly Father do also unto you, if ye from your hearts forgive not every one his brother their trespasses."

Matthew 18:23-35

OFFENDERS	DATE FORGIVEN	TREASURES I CAN VOLUNTARILY INVEST

5. Ask forgiveness for your offenses

MY OFFENSES	WORDING	DATE I ASKED FORGIVENESS

A PAGE OF REMEMBRANCE

When I asked individuals to forgive me, they responded to me with the following words and actions:

Answers to Quiz 3

1. Yes   God only promises that things will go well for us if we honor father and mother. (See Ephesians 6:1.)

2. Yes   Rejection of parents produces spiritural darkness that will affect every other relationship. "Whoso curseth his father or his mother, his lamp shall be put out in obscure darkness" (Proverbs 20:20).

3. Yes   Looking lustfully at the opposite sex is mental adultery. It will carry the same destruction into the marriage relationship. (See Matthew 5:28.)

4. No   These verses are not a permission for divorce as much as they are a regulation for existing practices. They are also superseded by Deuteronomy 22:29.

5. No   They damage compatibility and communication because they create guilt, distrust, wrong focus, and self-condemnation. (See Galatians 6:7-8.)

6. No   God judges pride swifter than immorality as in the case of instant death to Herod and mental insanity to King Nebuchadnezzer. (See Acts 12:23; Daniel 4:30.)

7. Yes   Whenever God's order is damaged, others are affected. One reason God hates divorce in Malachi 2:14 is its effect on the children.

8. No   In fact, God clearly teaches that going to the divorce court proves a lack of love. It would be better to suffer defrauding. (See I Corinthians 6:1-7.)

9. No   Because guilt is a function of the spirit. Books may give rationalizations to the mind but the spirit still condemns. (See Romans 2:15.)

10. No   Any appearances of temporary harmony are usually overcome by hidden or unexpected conflicts such as rejection by others, rivalry among children, comparison, and the need for justification. (See Proverbs 13:15.)

11. Yes But it must be done wisely and prayerfully. "He that covereth his sins shall not prosper, but whoso confesseth and forsaketh them shall have mercy" (Proverbs 28:13; see also James 5:16).

12. No It only begins the process. Usually time, changed attitudes, and loving actions are required to bring healing. (See Proverbs 18:19.)

13. No A bitter person's focus is not on his attitude but on the faults of others. He calls bitterness "hurts" or "disappointment," but his neighbor can detect bitterness. (See Proverbs 18:17.)

14. Yes Bitterness involves judging and condemning. When we do that, we stand guilty of doing the same thing. (See Romans 2:1–3.)

15. Yes God clearly teaches this in I John 4:20: ". . . For he that loveth not his brother whom he hath seen, how can he love God whom he hath not seen?"

16. No A bitter focus causes us to make that person a standard of comparison and establishes an emotional bondage that produces similar attitudes if not similar action. (See Matthew 7:1.)

17. No The words of a talebearer separate chief friends. They cause wounds and defilement. (See Proverbs 26:22; James 3:6.)

18. Yes God works through others. He even worked through wicked Shimei to curse David. (See II Samuel 16:11.)

19. No Even the perfect marriage and environment of Adam and Eve was destroyed through discontent. Satan convinced them that they were missing something. (See Genesis 3:1–7.)

20. Yes   God even described the types of struggles: the wife desiring to control her husband, the husband being domineering, pressure in making a living, and pain in childbearing. (See Genesis 3:16-17.)

21. No   Love covers by going beyond forgiveness and giving something of value to your enemy. (See Matthew 6:21; 5:40.)

22. No   Bitterness will show through tell-tale signs in your physical, emotional, and spiritual functioning. (See Hebrews 12:15.)

23. No   A person may experience anger and deal with it. (See Ephesians 4:26.) But, bitterness is a continuation and deepening of anger. (See Colossians 3:8.)

24. No   Forgiveness is not the same as pardon. Even God does not free the believer from the consequences of sin. He forgave David, but the consequences of his sin continued. (See II Samuel 12:11.)

Personal Commitment and Accountability

In rebuilding a clear conscience and a forgiving spirit:

☐ 1. I have purposed to maintain a conscience void of offense toward God and toward man.

☐ 2. As a first step toward this, I have purposed to clear my conscience with each person whom I have offended.

☐ 3. I have purposed that clearing my conscience will be only a beginning for God-given relationships.

☐ 4. I have purposed to maintain a forgiving spirit toward those who offend me.

☐ 5. I have purposed to relate God's forgiveness to God's great mercy to me.

☐ 6. I have purposed to develop a loving spirit toward offenders by investing in their lives.

☐ 7. I have purposed to examine myself in these areas each time that I am going to participate in the Lord's table at my church.

Signed _____ Date _____

GOAL NUMBER **4**

REBUILDING YOUR MARRIAGE AS FAR AS POSSIBLE

"And unto the married I command, yet not I, but the Lord, Let not the wife depart from her husband: But and if she depart, let her remain unmarried, or be reconciled to her husband: and let not the husband put away his wife."
I Corinthians 7:10-11

4 REBUILDER'S QUIZ

☐ ☐   1. Everyone who has a broken marriage should try to rebuild it.

☐ ☐   2. Once parents give their sons and daughters away in marriage their influence should be minimal in the marriage.

☐ ☐   3. The major cause of marital failure is incompatibility between partners.

☐ ☐   4. If a wife discovers that her husband is being unfaithful to her, she should confront him with the evidence as soon as possible.

☐ ☐   5. When a partner leaves and starts living immorally with someone else, there is little the other partner can do.

☐ ☐   6. Unless both partners work to put a marriage back together, it won't be put together.

☐ ☐   7. If a Christian couple marries, and later the husband wants a divorce, his wife should show submission by giving it to him.

☐ ☐   8. A husband who was divorced and remarried, could return to his first wife if the second wife died and the first wife had not remarried.

☐ ☐   9. If an adulterous partner refuses to repent, the other partner should just be patient and give more time.

☐ ☐   10. The basic needs of a husband and a wife are really the same since God gave us the same human nature.

See answers on pages 154–155.

Let us assume that a wife becomes bitter toward her husband, packs her bags, moves out, and begins living with another man.

What Scriptural steps should the husband take to be reconciled to her?

1. Spend time seeking after God

Study and complete Rebuilder's Goal Number One, pages 9-35.

2. Be committed to a vow of no divorce and no remarriage

Study and complete Rebuilder's Goal Number Two, pages 37-69.

3. Do not begin dating anyone else

Make it known that you do not intend to date anyone else, and that you are not even interested in looking around. Any dating that you do will only confirm to your former partner that you did not truly love him or her, because genuine love never fades or gives up hope. (See I Corinthians 13:7.) Dating jeopardizes the possibility of restoring the first marriage and often prompts the former partner to give up hope for reconciliation; he or she will then be more inclined to seek a new marriage. Dating by a divorced person clearly says, "I am really more interested in meeting my own needs than I am in reconciling my former marriage relationship."

4. Clear your conscience

Study and complete Rebuilder's Goal Number Three, pages 71-91.

5. Fully forgive your partner

Study and complete Rebuilder's Goal Number Four, pages 92-107.

6. Strengthen communication with your parents and relatives

One key to rebuilding a marriage is to involve the extended family: parents, parents-in-law, grandparents, brothers, and sisters. As many members of the family as possible should be involved in rebuilding a fractured marriage and in giving support to the children during a time when they are separated from a parent.

It is especially important to build better communication with the parents-in-law. Ask for their forgiveness. Bring the children to their home during times of visitation privileges. Show your genuine concern for their son or daughter. Ask them to help you understand the full extent of your offense in the marriage. One reason for doing this is that well-meaning parents-in-law often discourage their son or daughter from pursuing it any further.

One of the most important ways for the extended family to be involved in rebuilding a marriage is by setting aside special times for fasting and prayer. Each family member should examine his or her attitudes and then meet together in order to call upon God to bless the family. Marvelous results have occurred when this has been done.

7. Expect rebuilding to take time

Remember, "A brother [former partner] offended is harder to be won than a strong [walled] city: and their contentions are like the bars of a castle" (Proverbs 18:19). There were three ways to conquer a walled city. The first way was to climb over the walls. This was often a bloody ordeal that ended in failure. The second method was to lay siege to the city and wait. This required much patience, but it let the city know that its pursuers were sincere. The third way was to watch for an unexpected opening in the wall.

A patient partner will usually see a door open unexpectedly, if he or she is watching for it. One man waited three years for such an opportunity. During those years he faithfully visited his children and fulfilled his financial responsibility to his family. One day a problem developed with one of the children; and while working out the problem, he was reunited with his wife.

An offended wife will usually try to discern what her husband's motives are when he does something for her. She will try to determine whether he is doing it because:

- he feels guilty;
- he feels obligated;
- he wants something from her;
- he is concerned about his reputation;
- he was told by someone else to do it; or
- he is looking for illustrations to use in counseling his friends.

Her spirit will react negatively to any of these motivations. She wants him to do things for her as a sincere gesture of his own love. She wants his actions to grow spontaneously out of his own love and creativity. Above all, she wants him to be honest before God and explain what God is trying to teach him in his own spiritual growth.

8. Understand how defeat occurred in your partner's life

God has established authority as a protective covering for each Christian. Satan will do all he can to draw us out from under God-ordained authority. When we rebel, we expose ourselves to the realm and the power of Satan's control. (See I Samuel 15:23.)

Satan's temptation

Defeat in parent's life

Protection of authority   Power of Satan

- Sin nature
- Sins of foreparents
- Self will

- Lust of the flesh →
- Lust of the eyes →
- Pride of life →

9. Learn how to free your partner from sin's power

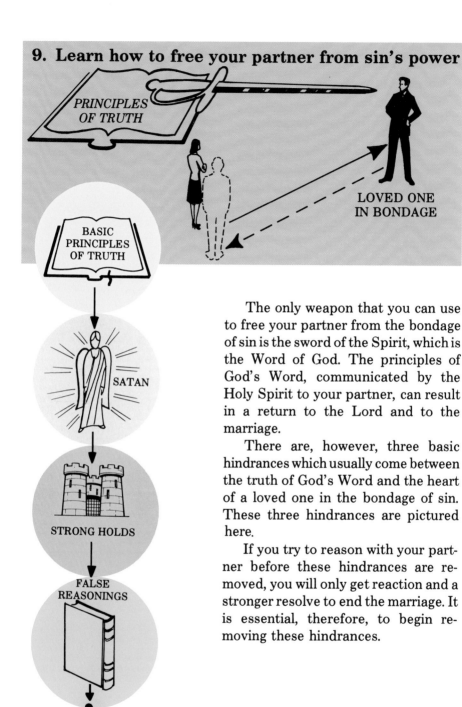

PRINCIPLES OF TRUTH

LOVED ONE IN BONDAGE

BASIC PRINCIPLES OF TRUTH

SATAN

STRONG HOLDS

FALSE REASONINGS

The only weapon that you can use to free your partner from the bondage of sin is the sword of the Spirit, which is the Word of God. The principles of God's Word, communicated by the Holy Spirit to your partner, can result in a return to the Lord and to the marriage.

There are, however, three basic hindrances which usually come between the truth of God's Word and the heart of a loved one in the bondage of sin. These three hindrances are pictured here.

If you try to reason with your partner before these hindrances are removed, you will only get reaction and a stronger resolve to end the marriage. It is essential, therefore, to begin removing these hindrances.

God has given mighty weapons to destroy each of these hindrances. "For though we walk in the flesh, we do not war after the flesh: (For the weapons of our warfare are . . . mighty through God to the pulling down of strong holds;) Casting down imaginations, and every high thing that exalteth itself against the knowledge of God, and bringing into captivity every thought to the obedience of Christ" (II Corinthians 10:3-5).

The first spiritual weapon to use is a prayer to bind Satan and build a "hedge of thorns" around your partner.

BASIC PRINCIPLES OF TRUTH

BIND SATAN

PRAY A "HEDGE" OF THORNS

CAST DOWN FALSE REASONINGS

CONQUER EVERY WRONG THOUGHT

TESTIMONIES OF THE POWER OF PRAYING A "HEDGE OF THORNS"

"The very next morning after learning how to pray a 'hedge of thorns,' I prayed it around several situations that seemed impossible for me to handle in our church. God answered three of the four within the day and gave unbelievable evidence of working in the fourth. Praise the Lord! At last a spiritual weapon with a punch against Satan that will prove to a skeptical world how great our God is!"

Pastor from Maryland

My brother had been divorced and was about to get remarried. I prayed a 'hedge of thorns' around him. In about a week and a half, I got a call one morning from my mother telling me that my brother and the girl were breaking it off. Today, he is back with his wife. Do I use that 'hedge' prayer with others? You better believe it!"

Pastor from Wisconsin

"Last year we received the 'hedge of thorns' material. My father-in-law and mother-in-law were divorced. After my mother-in-law attended the Basic Seminar, she asked God to forgive her for her divorce. She then asked my father-in-law's forgiveness. He did not receive her repentance. He was living with another woman at the time. My wife and I prayed a 'hedge of thorns' around my father-in-law, and less than ten days passed before the woman moved out. For almost a year we kept the hedge in place by prayer. During that time he could not keep a girl friend. Soon he asked my mother-in-law to go out with him. To make a long story short, three weeks ago they were remarried. To God be the glory!

"The 'hedge of thorns' has worked in every case in my church ministry. The only time that it has failed is when the mate has refused to receive the partner back or has not spoken 'comfortably' with the partner."

Pastor from Tennessee

PREREQUISITES FOR PRAYING A "HEDGE OF THORNS"

1. Salvation

This prayer can only be effectively used by a Christian. If you are not sure that you are a Christian, you can make sure by praying the following prayer:

"O God, thank You for loving me enough to send Your Son to die for me. I confess that I am a sinner, and I do now receive the living Lord Jesus Christ as my Savior. Cleanse me through His blood and make me Your child from this moment forward. (Based on Romans 3:23; 5:8; and 10:9.)

2. Victory over sin

God warns that if we regard iniquity in our hearts, He will not hear us. (See Psalm 66:18.) We do not gain victory by our own efforts but by entering into Christ's victory and using the engrafted truths of Romans 6 and 8 when temptation comes. (See Goal Number One, pages 22-28.)

3. A clear conscience

In order for a partner to be won back, that partner should have pleasant memories to associate with you. Bitter memories will convince the partner that anything is better than returning to you. For this reason, it is essential for you to ask your partner to free you from the blame and hurts of your past failures.

THE PRAYER TO BIND SATAN AND BUILD A "HEDGE OF THORNS"

"Heavenly Father, I ask You to rebuke[1] and bind Satan in the name and through the blood of the Lord Jesus Christ.[2]

"I ask You to build a 'hedge of thorns' around my partner, so that anyone with wrong influence will lose interest in him (or her) and leave.[3]

"I base this prayer on the command of Your Word[4] which states, 'What therefore God hath joined together, let not man put asunder.'[5]

"Thank You for hearing and answering my prayer."[6]

1. See Mark 3;27, Jude 1:9. Before we attempt to reclaim a loved one who has come under Satan's power, we must first bind Satan. Otherwise, he works through that loved one to create a reaction toward every attempt of restoration. Even though we have the spiritual authority in Christ to rebuke Satan, it is not wise to develop conversation with Satan, but rather to follow the example of Michael in asking God to rebuke him. This keeps our focus on the Lord and allows us to conquer through Him.

2. See John 14:13-14. Christ assured us that if we ask anything according to His name, He will do it so "that the Father may be glorified in the Son."

3. See Hosea 2:5-7. Gomer was the adulterous wife of the prophet Hosea. In order to restore her to her husband, God said that He would put a "hedge of thorns" around her. She would then lose her way, her lovers would lose interest in her, and she would decide to return to her husband.

4. See I John 5:14. The power of this prayer has its basis in the Word of God. We know that whatever is taught in His Word is according to His will. "And this is the confidence that we have in him, that, if we ask any thing according to his will, he heareth us."

5. See Matthew 19:6. This is the particular truth of Scripture that we are claiming in this prayer.

6. See I John 5:15. We know that God heard this prayer, because it is according to His stated will.

WHAT WILL HAPPEN WHEN YOU PRAY THIS PRAYER

Three things will begin to happen when you pray a "hedge of thorns" around your unfaithful partner:

1. He or she will become confused and lose direction.

   ". . . I will hedge up thy way with thorns, and make a wall, that she shall not find her paths" (Hosea 2:6).

2. Any other "lovers" will lose interest and leave.

   ". . . She shall follow after her lovers, but she shall not overtake them; and she shall seek them, but she shall not find them . . ." (Hosea 2:7a).

3. Troubles will motivate your partner to return.

   ". . . Then shall she say, I will go and return to my first husband; for then was it better with me than now" (Hosea 2:7b).

The scope and limitation of the "hedge of thorns" prayer

- This prayer binds the power of Satan and makes wrong influences ineffective.

- This prayer is *not* guaranteed to change the will of your partner once these influences are removed.

- It is, therefore, imperative that you follow through on the further instructions of Hosea 2:14-16 in order to win your partner back to God's ways.

GOMER

Gomer was the wife of the prophet Hosea. She was an adulterous wife. In this account, God gives us a graphic illustration of how the "hedge of thorns" works (Hosea 2:6-16).

SIX ESSENTIAL STEPS TO FOLLOW AFTER PRAYING THE "HEDGE OF THORNS"

5

1. **Design a special time to be together with your partner.**

   "Therefore, behold, I will allure her, and bring her into the wilderness . . ." (Hosea 2:14).

2. **Speak gentle, loving words of acceptance and reassurance.**

   ". . . And [I will] speak comfortably unto her." (Hosea 2:14).

3. **Identify basic needs and discuss how you plan to meet them.**

   "And I will give her her vineyards from thence . . ." (Hosea 2:15).

4. **Turn the scars of defeat and failure into a life message that will give hope and direction to others.**

   "And [I will give] the valley of Achor [trouble] for a door of hope . . ." (Hosea 2:15).

5. **Reaffirm your commitment to the marriage covenant.**

   "And I will betroth thee unto me for ever; yea, I will betroth thee unto me in righteousness, and in judgment, and in lovingkindness, and in mercies" (Hosea 2:19).

6. **Pull down false reasonings and teach the basic truths of God's Word.**

   ". . . And thou shalt know the Lord" (Hosea 2:20).

   This final step is the most important of all. Without it, Satan will be free to take your partner captive once again. The purpose of binding Satan, building a "hedge," and restoring fellowship is to give you an opportunity to build the principles of God's Word into the life of your partner.

SEVEN BASIC PRINCIPLES TO BUILD INTO THE LIFE OF YOUR PARTNER

1. Self-acceptance

Satan hates the body of a Christian. He wants us to despise, reject, and misuse it. However, God wants us to accept our bodies as being made in His image, as temples of the Holy Spirit, and as weapons of righteousness as we yield them to God. (See Genesis 1:27; I Corinthians 6:19; Romans 6:13.)

2. Submission to authority

God has provided authority as an umbrella of protection and a means of counsel and direction. By staying under that umbrella, we escape destructive temptations. (See Romans 13:1-6; I Timothy 6:1; I Corinthians 11:3.)

3. Clear conscience

God warns that, if we do not have a clear conscience, we will make shipwreck of our faith. Guilt allows Satan to condemn us and make us a prey to evil men.   (See I Timothy 1:19; Romans 8:1; II Timothy 3:6.)

4. A forgiving spirit

No relationship can survive a wounded spirit. It will defile each person and destroy communication. (See Hebrews 12:15; Matthew 6:15.)

5. Yielding rights

The very basis of marriage is the yielding of personal rights. This action is the result of meekness and opens up a wealth of God's promises to those who have it. (See Matthew 5:5; I Peter 3:4; Philippians 2:5-8.)

6. Moral freedom

If your partner is not freed from the power of lustful habits, he or she will be drawn back under the power of Satan. It is vital that the principles of moral freedom be explained, demonstrated, and learned so that there can be new power to live in harmony with God's standards. (See Galatians 6:6-7; I Thessalonians 4:3-8.)

7. The power of being in Christ

None of these principles can be lived out in our own energy. Christ's power within us must achieve them. We experience His power by knowing that we died with Christ, reckoning ourselves dead to sin, and yielding our members as instruments of righteousness to God. It would be very important to study the material on pages 22-28 with your partner so that together you can engraft God's Word into your souls and be accountable to each other for its daily application. (See Romans 6, 7, 8.)

7 STEPS TO TAKE IF YOUR PARTNER CONTINUES TO BE REBELLIOUS

1. Praying for a "hedge of thorns" is most effective when it is done by one who is in direct authority. Thus, a parent or husband will have more influence in praying for a "hedge of thorns" around an adulterous wife than a friend of the family will have. A pastor will have more authority in praying for a "hedge of thorns" than a member in the church will have.

2. If you discover after praying for a "hedge of thorns" that your partner is not being influenced by Satan's power or by wrong friends, but by his own willful rejection of truth, then you must remove the "hedge of protection" and allow the Lord to carry out further discipline. (See Hebrews 3:7-10; Matthew 19:8.)

3. Paul removed the "hedge of protection" from an immoral man in the Corinthian church. Paul delivered him over to Satan for the destruction of fleshly desires so that he could turn from sin and respond to God's grace. (See I Corinthians 5:5.)

4. Job was a righteous man. He regularly prayed for a "hedge" around his seven sons and three daughters. This "hedge" was so effective that Satan complained about it. "Hast not thou made a hedge about him, and about his house, and about all that he hath on every side? thou hast blessed the work of his hands, and his substance is increased in the land" (Job 1:10).

   There is evidence, however, that Job's children, of their own will, began to curse God in their hearts. Eventually, the "hedge of protection" was removed by God, and Satan was given freedom to bring physical destruction to them.

Scriptural Basis for Removing the "Hedge of Protection"

Job feared that his sons and daughters were cursing God in their heart, so he interceded for them. He was a perfect and upright man and God "made an hedge about him, and about his house, and about all that he hath on every side" (Job 1:10).

- *Ephesians 6:1; Deuteronomy 21:18-21*

    God expects parents to discipline their sons and daughters as much as they possibly can.

- *I Corinthians 11:29-30; Hebrews 12:6; 13:7*

    God expects the church to to carry out discipline when a son or daughter rebels against the parents.

- *Romans 13:1-6*

    God has given power to the government to punish evildoers when the laws are violated.

JOB

ADDITIONAL TESTIMONIES OF THE EFFECTIVENESS OF THE "HEDGE OF THORNS"

"I sat here this week teary-eyed through much of what you had to say. The reason why is simple. I know I wouldn't be sitting here at all if it were not for the 'hedge' my husband prayed around me a year ago! I was rebellious and caught up in a strong deception and delusion and wanted no part of my husband or God.

"When my adulterous situation fell apart, I was crushed and could not understand what had happened. But I praise God now from the depth of my being and spirit for the true love and faithfulness of my husband in praying that 'hedge' around me. I know that his faith and the grace of God are the only things that snatched me out of the jaws of the roaring lion that seeks to devour all marriages. I thank God that our pastor would not compromise in his determination that our marriage *could be saved,* and that he shared this powerful, powerful promise and weapon with my husband.

Because he did and God is faithful, I sit here today *beside my husband,* with my brother and his wife (who has just returned to him because a 'hedge' was prayed around her); and we're now praying for a 'hedge' around an uncle who has *left the ministry* for another woman! Please keep teaching the truth of God and the *power* of praying this 'hedge of thorns'!!! God richly bless your ministry."

A wife from Los Angeles

"Four weeks ago I left my wife, at which time I was a backsliding Christian. Not long after, she found a boyfriend and told me that she wanted a divorce. She said that the hurts in our marriage were too great for reconciliation. Yesterday, I prayed for a 'hedge of thorns' around her and last night I had a talk with her. Her boyfriend was there in our home during our talk. She told her boyfriend to leave and said that she loves me and wants me home. All praise to God."

A husband from Los Angeles

"Three weeks ago, my two assistants and I prayed for a 'hedge of thorns' around a few men in the church who had left their wives and were living in sin. Yesterday, one of these men called and asked to speak with me. I told him of his need for a Savior and Lord. He told me he needed a wife who would stop listening to wrong friends. I told him that when he was born again, he could pray for a 'hedge of thorns' around his wife so that her wrong friends would leave. When he asked me what a 'hedge of thorns' was, I opened my Bible to Hosea and showed him what God had to say.

"He turned white, jabbed his finger onto those verses and said, 'That's what happened to me.' He told me how he no longer could look at his girlfriend without seeing the Lord shaking His head 'No.' He told me how this girl, who was so lovely, had begun to look ugly to him in recent days. He began to cry as he said, 'There is power in this Book.' A few moments later, he prayed a prayer of repentance. He is now a new man. He is into the Word and has committed himself to using God's principles to restore his marriage."

A pastor from New York

VICTORY EVEN WHEN THE PARTNER DOES NOT RETURN

"My pastor helped me to pray for a 'hedge of thorns' around my ex-husband. He told me to be sure to do anything that the Holy Spirit prompted me to do during that month before my ex-husband's wedding. I made contact with him by phone several times. I was careful to be gentle and show gratitude. During those talks he even shared with me those things which deeply hurt him during our marriage. I prayed day and night.

"On September fourth they were married. Some may say this is an example of God's failure. Of course it's not! God was well able to stop that marriage. Philippians 4:19 promises God will supply my needs. He has. Though words can not describe the pain I felt when a babysitter said, 'He's on his honeymoon,' immediately I had peace. The same loving God who saved me is now my 'husband.' He never misses church, He never makes a mess of our finances, He never leaves me to go off to do other things, He never changes. I don't mind being broken to help others be revived for God."

A rebuilder from Kansas City

Be prepared to continue having genuine love and forgiveness for your former partner, even if he or she remarries. Sometimes a person remarries in order to discourage the persistent pressure of the first partner. This is why you must fully commit the entire matter to the Lord and trust Him to work out His best in your life and marriage. As we understand that God's ultimate purpose is to build in us the character of the Lord Jesus Christ, we can be confident that ". . . all things work together for good to them that love God, to them who are the called according to his purpose . . . to be conformed to the image of His Son . . ." (Romans 8:28-29).

WHEN YOUR PARTNER RETURNS . . .

IDENTIFY AND MEET BASIC NEEDS

SEVEN BASIC NEEDS OF A HUSBAND

I. A HUSBAND NEEDS A WIFE WHO RESPECTS HIM AS A MAN

How does a wife destroy her husband's manliness?

A. BY EXPECTING HIM TO KNOW WHAT PROTECTION YOU NEED

1. Physical
2. Spiritual
3. Mental
4. Emotional

- *Tell your husband how he can protect you.*

B. BY BEING FINANCIALLY INDEPENDENT

1. Love is killed by self-sufficiency.
2. Whoever controls the money controls the leadership.

- *Center your work and your ministry in your home.*

C. BY GREATER LOYALTY TO OUTSIDE LEADERSHIP

1. Pastor and church leaders
2. Men and women Bible teachers
3. Relatives and friends

- *Ask your husband your spiritual questions. (See I Corinthians 14:35.)*

D. BY RESISTING HIS DECISIONS IN YOUR SPIRIT

1. A wife's spirit controls her husband's ambitions.
2. Reviewing past failure destroys a husband's self-worth.

* *Learn how to wisely appeal to your husband.*

E. BY RESISTING HIS PHYSICAL AFFECTION

1. This is the unspoken crushing of a man's spirit.
2. A wife's Godliness is a powerful guard against her husband's abuse of her. (See I Peter 3:1.)

* *Learn the power of prayer based on Scripture. (See James 5:16.)*

F. BY TAKING MATTERS INTO YOUR OWN HANDS

1. When a wife intrudes into one responsibility, her husband often surrenders other responsibilities as well.
2. A wife may avoid temporary consequences, but cause ultimate destruction. (See Proverbs 14:1.)

* *Do not become your husband's conscience. Wisely appeal wrong decisions; then give him room to fail.*

II. A HUSBAND NEEDS A WIFE WHO ACCEPTS HIM AS A LEADER AND BELIEVES IN HIS GOD-GIVEN RESPONSIBILITIES

What are the basic needs of a leader?

A. REASSURANCE THAT HIS AUTHORITY COMES FROM GOD

1. Husbands are commanded to govern their wives. (See Genesis 3:16.)
2. Wives are commanded to submit to their husbands. (See Ephesians 5:22; Colossians 3:18; I Peter 3:1.)
3. A wife's submission qualifies her husband for church leadership. (See I Timothy 3:4-5.)
4. The headship of the husband is illustrated in Christ and the Church. (See I Corinthians 11:3.)

* *Reassure your husband that he is your God-given leader.*

B. CONFIDENCE THAT GOD IS WORKING THROUGH HIM

1. God works through a man's decisions, whether they are good or bad.
2. Bad decisions reveal a man's needs and allow the wife to appeal and demonstrate Godly character.
3. The more a wife trusts her husband, the more careful he will be in giving her direction.

- *When your husband makes a bad decision, explain to him how God is using it to benefit your spiritual life.*

C. LOYALTY WHEN MISTAKES ARE MADE AND PRESSURES INCREASE

1. Loyalty can only be demonstrated in adversity.
2. A husband's trust in his wife is often misinterpreted as taking her for granted.

- *Never ask others for counsel without your husband's approval.*

D. ADMIRATION FOR LEADERSHIP ON A LARGER BASIS (SEE PSALM 15.)

1. When he walks uprightly
2. When he works righteousness
3. When he speaks truth in his heart
4. When he refuses to gossip
5. When he does no evil to his neighbor
6. When he does not take up offenses
7. When he rejects those who are evil
8. When he honors Godly men
9. When he keeps promises
10. When he does not profit by others' misfortunes
11. When he refuses to accept a bribe

- *Write out illustrations of these leadership qualities.*

E. PRAISE FOR ANY QUALITIES OF A CHURCH LEADER (SEE I TIMOTHY 3:2-8.)

1. Clear conscience
2. One wife
3. Spiritual alertness
4. Wisdom
5. Modesty
6. Hospitality
7. Desire to teach
8. Not deceived by wine
9. Hard worker
10. Generous
11. Patient
12. Peacemaker
13. Not covetous
14. A good manager of his family
15. A maturing Christian
16. A good reputation

- *Let your husband hear you praise him to others.*

F. ENCOURAGEMENT NOT TO GIVE UP GOD-GIVEN GOALS

1. A man demonstrates manliness when he fulfills God-given responsibility.
2. Expect the birth, death, and fulfillment of visions.

- *Encourage your husband to verbalize his deepest wishes.*

G. PATIENCE DURING TIMES OF PRESSURE

1. A man's goals often involve long-range achievement.
2. A wife's needs usually involve immediate projects.

- *Accept difficult situations from God without giving Him a deadline to remove them.*

H. ENTHUSIASM FOR HIS ACHIEVEMENTS

1. Rejection of a husband's achievement is rejection of him.
2. Sharing his excitement is more important than sharing his work.

- *Review the benefits which his leadership has already provided.*

I. ATTENTIVENESS WHEN HE IS TALKING

- *Look at your husband admiringly when he talks to others, as this will inspire their respect.*

III. A HUSBAND NEEDS A WIFE WHO WILL CONTINUE TO DEVELOP INWARD AND OUTWARD BEAUTY

How can you become more of the wife of your husband's dreams?

A. HAIR—SYMBOL OF BEING UNDER AUTHORITY (SEE I CORINTHIANS 11:10.)

1. Hair "is given her for a covering." (See I Corinthians 11:15.)
2. Hair is a basis for spiritual protection. (See I Corinthians 11:10.)
3. Hair is a woman's glory. (See I Corinthians 11:15.)
4. Hair style must reflect the husband's wishes. (See Ephesians 5:24.)

   a. Femininity vs. Masculinity
   b. Contentment vs. Frustration
   c. Neatness vs. Carelessness
   d. Submission vs. Pride
   e. Diligence vs. Weariness
   f. Softness vs. Hardness
   g. Self-acceptance vs. Self-rejection
   h. Obedience vs. Defiance
   i. Patience vs. Impatience
   j. Personal Organization vs. Disorganization
   k. Personal Discipline vs. Inconsistency

   - *Spend extra time and effort on your appearance, because it is an expression of reverence.*
   - *Discover and conform to your husband's real wishes regarding your appearance..*

B. DRESS—SYMBOL OF HUSBAND'S TASTE, STANDARDS, AND PROVISIONS

1. Modesty is always in style.
2. A wife should dress to please her husband.
3. A wife's dress should draw attention to her countenance.

   - *Remember that what your husband likes, he enjoys seeing often.*

C. CARE OF CLOTHES IS A SYMBOL OF GRATEFULNESS

   - *Eliminate unused clothes from your wardrobe.*

D. HOME—SYMBOL OF HUSBAND'S WISDOM, PROVISION, AND PROTECTION

1. A man's message is determined by what happens in his home. (See I Timothy 3:4.)
2. Convictions and character are formed in the home.
3. A wife's spirit sets the atmosphere in the home.

- *Keep the home free of clutter.*
- *Train the children to be neat and clean.*
- *Provide good music throughout the day.*
- *Appeal wisely for needed home repairs.*

E. WEIGHT—SYMBOL OF HUSBAND'S LEADERSHIP AND WIFE'S SELF-CONTROL

1. God is concerned about overeating and overweight. (See Proverbs 23:21.)
2. Physical or spiritual causes can produce overweight.
3. Weight control requires consistent conformity to God's principles of living.

- *Let God and your husband know that you care about your weight.*
- *Dedicate your body as a living sacrifice to God. (See Romans 12:1.)*
- *Work on achievable goals together.*
- *Identify and remove hindrances to weight control.*

Bitterness	*Wrong mealtimes*
Wrong foods	*Medical problems*

F. A MEEK AND QUIET SPIRIT—BASIS OF A WIFE'S BEAUTY (SEE I PETER 3:1-7.)

1. Meekness is yielding rights.
2. A quiet spirit is conquering fear and worry.

- *Separate your rights from your responsibilities.*
- *Yield your rights and expectations to God.*
- *Visualize how Godly character can result from disappointments.*

G. POISE—SYMBOL OF HUSBAND'S TRAINING

1. Basis of poise is contentment. (See I Timothy 6:6.)
2. Basis of contentment is self-acceptance. (See Psalm 139:14.)

- *Be well-groomed so you are not self-conscious.*
- *Learn to communicate:*

  Acceptance   *Interest*
  Encouragement   *Understanding*
  Kindness   *Godly Standards*

IV. A HUSBAND NEEDS A WIFE WHO CAN LOVINGLY APPEAL TO HIM WHEN HE IS GOING BEYOND HIS LIMITATIONS AND WISELY RESPOND TO THOSE WHO QUESTION HIS IDEAS, GOALS, OR MOTIVES

What words, actions, or decisions should you appeal?

A. LEARN THE PRINCIPLES OF APPEALING TO GOD

1. Must be in right standing with God. (See Matthew 7:21.)
2. Must use right basis for appeal—His reputation, His goals, His authority. (See Matthew 6:9-13.)
3. Must have right timing. (See John 2:4.)
4. Must convey right attitudes. (See James 4:3.)
5. Must use right wording. (See John 4:24.)

- *Be sure you are a Christian. (See Romans 10:9-13.)*
- *Totally dedicate your life to God's will. (See Romans 12:1-2.)*
- *Do not condone any sin in your life. (See Psalm 66:18.)*
- *Be willing to sacrifice for the request you make.*

B. APPLY THESE SAME PRINCIPLES IN APPEALING TO YOUR HUSBAND

1. A husband's authority is defined and limited by God's Word.

   a. Exercise headship in his family. (See I Corinthians 11:3.)
   b. Love his wife as Christ loved the Church. (See Ephesians 5:25.)
   c. Teach his children Godly wisdom. (See Galatians 4:1-2.)
   d. Support his wife's discipline of the children. (See Proverbs 6:20.)
   e. Honor his wife as "weaker vessel" and "heirs together." (See I Peter 3:7.)
   f. Provide physical affection. (See I Corinthians 7:5.)

2. A wife's spirit can overcome her husband's resistance.

   - *Ask your husband to define your responsibilities.*
   - *Explain your needs and fears without condemning him.*
   - *After appealing, focus on the positive benefits, whatever happens.*

C. MAKE SURE YOUR ATTITUDES ARE CONSISTENTLY RIGHT

1. Attitudes must demonstrate genuine love. (See I Corinthians 13:2-8.)
2. Attitudes must demonstrate loyalty. (See Ruth 1:16-17.)
3. Attitudes must demonstrate a servant's heart. (See Philippians 2:1-11.)

   - *Ask your husband to tell you when you have a resistant spirit.*
   - *Ask forgiveness whenever this happens.*

D. DO NOT APPEASE REACTION BY DISCREDITING YOUR HUSBAND

1. Abigail's appeal to David discredited her husband. (See I Samuel 25:25.)
2. Those who react to your husband will often distort and misuse your words.

   - *Dispel a backbiting tongue by silence. (See Proverbs 26:20.)*

E. LEARN INSIGHTS FROM GODLY WOMEN IN SCRIPTURE

1. Sarah's obedient spirit (See I Peter 3:1-7.)
2. Esther's wise appeals (See Esther 5-9.)
3. Ruth's loyal spirit (See Ruth 1-4.)

V. A HUSBAND NEEDS TIME TO BE ALONE WITH THE LORD

A. GOD MADE MAN TO HAVE FELLOWSHIP WITH HIM FIRST

1. Adam walked with God before his wife was created.
2. Isaac meditated in the field before his wife was provided.
3. A man's success is based on seeking after God. (See II Chronicles 26:5.)

   - *Share questions and decisions that require your husband to seek the Lord.*

B. THE RICHER A MAN'S FELLOWSHIP IS WITH GOD, THE SWEETER A MAN'S FELLOWSHIP WILL BE WITH HIS WIFE

1. When a man is out of fellowship with God, he will be out of fellowship with his wife and children.
2. A man's love for God is reflected in his love for Scripture.

   - *Tell your husband how pleased you are when you see him spending time with the Lord.*

C. EVERY MAN NEEDS HIS OWN "BETHEL"

1. A Bethel is a private meeting place with God. (See Genesis 31:13.)
2. A Bethel can be a little room indoors or a quiet place outdoors. (See Matthew 6:6.)

   - *Encourage your husband to find a private place in which to meet God.*

D. A MAN'S DESIRE TO BE ALONE IS NOT A REJECTION OF HIS WIFE

1. Times alone allow a husband to regain a broader perspective.
2. Discussions with other men sharpen his thinking. (See Proverbs 27:17.)

   • *Increase your prayers for your husband when he is alone with the Lord.*

E. EVERY MAN MUST "BEAR HIS OWN BURDEN" (SEE GALATIANS 6:5.)

1. Man was made to work best under pressure.
2. Lessons he learns can be shared with wife and children. (See II Corinthians 1:4-8.)
3. Heavy burdens should be shared. (See Galatians 6:2.)

   • *Appeal to husband to share burdens that affect his spirit over long periods of time.*

F. DO NOT ASSUME YOU CAUSED HIS BURDEN OR ARE RESPONSIBLE TO REMOVE IT

VI. A HUSBAND NEEDS A WIFE WHO IS GRATEFUL FOR ALL HE HAS DONE AND IS DOING FOR HER

What are the basic aspects of gratefulness?

A. GIVING ALL YOUR EXPECTATIONS TO GOD (SEE PSALM 62:5.)

1. Expectations destroy gratefulness.
2. Gratefulness is the basis of happiness. A happy wife is a crown to her husband. An unhappy wife is a public rebuke to him.
3. Men are attracted to grateful women.
4. A husband may try to decrease his wife's expectations by giving her less.

  • *Expect nothing and be genuinely grateful for each little evidence of your husband's love.*

B. LEARNING CONTENTMENT WITH GODLINESS (SEE I TIMOTHY 6:6.)

1. Set your affections on things above. (See Colossians 3:1.)

God the Father	Heaven
All authority	True wisdom
The souls of others	The Word of God
The Lord Jesus Christ	Rejoicing angels
True riches	

2. Trade temporal things to win more of Christ. (See Philippians 3:7-8.)

  a. Realize that "things" compete with Christ.
  b. Offer to God all things in exchange for more of Christ.
  c. Rejoice when God takes anything, knowing you will get back more in return.

C. LISTING WHAT YOUR HUSBAND IS DOING FOR YOU IN ORDER OF THEIR IMPORTANCE TO HIM

1. A wife's priorities are usually different from a husband's.
2. A husband's priorities usually involve activities and expenditures to build his reputation and to provide security.

  • *Help your husband gain Scriptural self-acceptance.*

D. LISTING WHAT YOUR HUSBAND HAS WISELY NOT DONE

1. A wife often overlooks the mistakes and failures her husband has avoided.
2. Specific praise increases a man's self-image.

   • *Praise your husband for any achievement in areas where you want him to excel.*

E. SEEING HOW ALL THINGS WORK TOGETHER FOR GOOD

1. God promises that all things work together for good. (See Romans 8:28.)
2. Tribulation can produce the character of Christ in us.
3. For Godly character we must love God and purpose to do His will.

   • *Memorize the fruits of the spirit in Galatians 5:22-23. Visualize how the struggles and joys of your marriage are helping you achieve these qualities.*

VII. A HUSBAND NEEDS A WIFE WHO WILL BE PRAISED BY OTHER PEOPLE FOR HER CHARACTER AND HER GOOD WORKS

Let your light so shine . . .

A. HER SPIRITUAL LEADERS SHOULD PRAISE HER

For knowing them and their need (See I Thessalonians 5:12-13.)
For her wisdom and discretion (See Titus 2:4; Proverbs 31:26.)
For her love for husband and children (See Titus 2:4.)
For her submission and obedience to husband (See Titus 2:5; I Timothy 3:4; Ephesians 5:22; I Peter 3:1.)
For her high morals (See Titus 2:5.)
For her home management (See Titus 2:5; Proverbs 31.)

B. HER CHILDREN SHOULD PRAISE HER

"Rise up and call her Blessed"
For her virtue (See Proverbs 31:10.)
For her harmony with her husband (See Proverbs 31:11-12.)
For her diligence, thriftiness, and wise home management
   (See Proverbs 31.)
For her alertness and skill in meeting her children's needs
   (See Proverbs 31.)
For her wisdom and kindness (See Proverbs 31:26.)

C. HER GOVERNMENT LEADERS SHOULD PRAISE HER

For her prayers for them (See I Timothy 2:1-5.)
For her good works (See Proverbs 31:31.)

D. HER NEIGHBORS SHOULD PRAISE HER

For her generosity to the poor and needy (See Proverbs 31:20.)
For hospitality to visitors (See I Timothy 5:10.)
For relieving the afflicted (See I Timothy 5:10.)

E. HER CHURCH SHOULD PRAISE HER

For submitting to her husband and thus not blaspheming
God's Word (See Titus 2:5.)
For her practical care of the saints (See I Timothy 5:10.)
For her faithfulness to her marriage vows (See I Timothy 5:9.)
For her ability to teach younger women (See Titus 2:4.)

F. SPECIAL CAUTIONS

A wife's good works should demonstrate her husband's
sincere motives: giving to needs without expectation of
reward. (See Luke 14:12-14.)
A wife should not try to resolve her husband's problems
with good works without his consent.

SEVEN BASIC NEEDS OF A WIFE

I. SHE NEEDS THE STABILITY AND DIRECTION OF A SPIRITUAL LEADER

Every woman has certain needs which will only be met by strong spiritual leadership. Spiritual leadership is not only an indication of where a man is spiritually; it shows the direction in which he is going. There are four major marks of spiritual leadership that a wife looks for in her husband:

A. DESIRE TO SEEK THE LORD

Your wife needs to know that you delight in the Lord and are getting direction from Him. This comes from a consistent, growing relationship with the Lord.

- *List the evidences in your life that show a desire to seek the Lord:*
  - ☐ *Regular times in God's Word.*
  - ☐ *Consistent memorization of Scripture.*
  - ☐ *Faithfulness in prayer.*
  - ☐ *Regular church attendance.*
  - ☐ *Reading Christian books.*
  - ☐ *Fellowship with sincere Christians.*
  - ☐ *Discussions of spiritual matters.*

B. CONVICTIONS BASED ON SCRIPTURE

As your wife sees you establishing God's standards in your life, she will be motivated to submit to your leadership and set similar standards in her own life.

- *List the evidences of Scriptural convictions which you have or purpose to have:*
  - ☐ *Demonstrating love for God by loving your wife, children, and others. (See I John 4:20.)*
  - ☐ *Avoiding actions or activities that might cause your wife, children, or others to stumble. (See Romans 14.)*
  - ☐ *Purposing to make your home a center of Godly learning and living. (See Psalm 101.)*
  - ☐ *Others.*

C. DETERMINATION TO FOLLOW CONVICTIONS

Consistent obedience to Scriptural standards provides the strength and example your wife needs to obey God and you.

- *List the obstacles which hinder you from consistently obeying God's standards. Determine steps to overcome them:*

  ☐ *Influence of and attention to TV.*
  ☐ *Influence of wrong friends.*
  ☐ *Losing temper.*
  ☐ *Wrong priorities.*
  ☐ *Guilt from past failures.*
  ☐ *Lack of wisdom.*
  ☐ *Bondage to enslaving habits.*
  ☐ *Pride and willfulness.*

D. LOVE IN WHATEVER IS DONE

The evidence of being led and motivated by God's Spirit is having the fruit of the Spirit in all your actions. The first fruit is love.

- *List the ways in which you are demonstrating love to your wife. Then ask her to explain which ones do or do not express love to her and why.*

II. SHE NEEDS TO KNOW THAT SHE IS MEETING VITAL NEEDS IN YOUR LIFE AND WORK THAT NO OTHER WOMAN CAN MEET

A wife must feel that she is very special to her husband. Telling her that she is special is not enough. She wants to know how she is special. God made her to be an "help meet" for her husband. The needs that a wife is meeting must be of importance to her husband. The more important they are, the more he will praise and appreciate her.

The most devastating action of a husband is to give one of his wife's special tasks to some other woman to do. Adding insult to injury would be to praise the other woman for doing it. The scourge of a woman is jealousy. Jealousy is the fear of being displaced.

The tendency of a man is to not share his real needs with his wife. He wants her to admire him as a success. But before honor must come humility. He will win her love more by sharing his specific failures than by reporting his successes. He must not only explain his needs but teach her precisely what she can do to help meet them.

- *List needs that your wife is now meeting that no other woman can meet.*

    1. *She is the basis of your most important message, which is the illustration of how Christ loves the Church.*
    2. *She provides the potential for power in your prayers. (See I Peter 3:7.)*
    3. *She is an "alarm system" against other women with wrong motives.*
    4. *She is a mirror of your present spiritual condition.*
    5. *She can give you the joy of a physical relationship without guilt. (See Proverbs 5:19-20.)*
    6. *She is a safeguard to your hasty decisions because of her need for security and consistency.*
    7. *She instills Godly attitudes in children.*
    8. *She discerns the real needs of the children.*

SPECIAL STEPS IN SELECTING A SECRETARY

1. MAKE SURE THAT THE SECRETARY YOU HIRE IS NOT LIKELY TO LOOK TO YOU TO MEET HER EMOTIONAL NEEDS

Attempting to meet the emotional needs of a secretary is certain to produce insecurity in your wife, if not jealousy and resentment. A secretary's basic emotional needs must be met by her parents if she is single, her husband if she is married, and God if she is widowed.

2. MAKE SURE THAT YOUR WIFE MEETS, INTERVIEWS, AND APPROVES OF THE SECRETARY BEFORE YOU HIRE HER.

Technically, a secretary is working for your wife, since she is doing things to assist you that your wife is not able to do.

3. KEEP YOUR RELATIONSHIP WITH YOUR SECRETARY ON A BUSINESS LEVEL AT ALL TIMES

Do not become involved in the personal life of your secretary. If she has serious problems, refer her to her husband, her parents, her minister, or other sources of help.

4. MAKE SURE THAT YOUR WIFE CAN CALL YOU WITHOUT GOING THROUGH YOUR SECRETARY

If you do not have a private phone, instruct the secretary to always put your wife through without asking questions. If you are busy, have her tell your wife what you are doing and let her make the decision of whether or not to disturb you.

5. MAKE SURE THAT YOU NEVER ASK YOUR SECRETARY TO MEET PERSONAL NEEDS OR PERFORM SPECIAL TASKS THAT YOUR WIFE NORMALLY DOES

Do not ask a secretary to sew a button on your coat or bake you a special pie. Do not allow her to bake a cake to celebrate your birthday.

6. MAKE SURE THAT YOUR SECRETARY IS COMMITTED TO THE SUCCESS OF YOUR MARRIAGE

Your secretary must help you to make your wife and home your priority by shielding you from unnecessary interruptions, helping you keep appointments with your wife, and guarding you from temptations of moral impurity.

7. MAKE SURE THAT YOU PRAISE YOUR WIFE TO YOUR SECRETARY AND NEVER DISCUSS PROBLEMS IN YOUR MARRIAGE WITH HER

Appreciate your secretary's abilities without praising her to your wife, especially if your wife does not have equal abilities in that area.

III. SHE NEEDS TO SEE AND HEAR THAT YOU CHERISH HER AND THAT YOU DELIGHT IN HER AS A PERSON

The key word here is to cherish your wife. Most men do not know what this means or how to do it. To cherish your wife is to see great value in her as a person, to protect her, and to praise her to others.

It is important for your wife to know that she is a vital part of your world. It is equally important for her to know that your delight in her goes beyond the things she can do for you.

- *List the character qualities and personality traits that first attracted you to your wife:*

  1. _____
  2. _____
  3. _____
  4. _____
  5. _____
  6. _____
  7. _____

She needs to hear you rehearse the character qualities, personality traits, and family qualities that attracted you to her and the evidences of God's leading that brought you together. She wants to know that these qualities are still important to you.

The growing proof that you cherish your wife is your ability to take unchangeable past experiences, physical features, and personality characteristics which she has difficulty accepting and turn them into praiseworthy attributes in her. As your wife learns to view these things from God's perspective, she will not only develop an inner radiance but also a significant life message.

IV. SHE NEEDS TO KNOW THAT YOU UNDERSTAND HER BY PROTECTING HER IN AREAS OF HER LIMITATIONS

Every wife has a deep need to be understood. Most men think that they understand their wives, but they may not.

Basic to understanding your wife is knowing that she wants boundaries that show a concern for her, not a neglect of her. She wants you to be aware of her spiritual, mental, emotional, and physical strengths and weaknesses and to have the wisdom and courage to provide loving but firm direction, so that she will not fail by going beyond her limitations. Occasionally your wife will ask you for something she does not really want. She is testing you to see if you are perceptive to her real needs and dangers. If you give her whatever she wants, she will become insecure.

Your first priority is to know your wife so well that you understand when to be firm and when to be lenient. Loving firmness is respected when you both know in your spirit that it is right. Your wife is very susceptible to any man who understands her and is frustrated with any man who does not—especially those who say they do but do not.

V. SHE NEEDS TO KNOW THAT YOU ENJOY SETTING ASIDE TIME FOR INTIMATE CONVERSATION WITH HER

Perhaps the most basic need of your wife is intimate communication. Intimate conversation is only possible when there is a oneness of spirit. This is the goal of a marriage.

When you come home, your wife has more things to talk about than you probably suspect. Her enjoyment of sharing them only comes if she knows that you enjoy listening and are not anxious to do something else. If she senses that you are preoccupied or in a hurry, she will not talk; or she will discuss only a few items of lesser importance. She is willing to make this "sacrifice" unless someone else calls or visits and talks about trivia to you. Then she reacts— especially if it's a woman.

The key to intimate conversation is having a regular time planned for it. Half of her enjoyment is anticipating these times. The ultimate level of intimate conversation occurs when your wife trusts you with the secrets of her deepest emotions.

- *List the regular time(s) you and your wife have for intimate conversation. (If none, plan one now.)*

- *List the places that your wife enjoys going in order to have intimate conversation.*

  ☐ *Breakfast at* _____
  ☐ *Shopping at* _____
  ☐ *Dinner at* _____
  ☐ *At home during* _____

- *List the distractions that hinder intimate conversation when you are together. Purpose to avoid them.*

  ☐ *Having your mind on other things.*
  ☐ *Phone calls.*
  ☐ *Being late for your appointment.*
  ☐ *Talking to friends you meet.*
  ☐ *Looking at other women.*
  ☐ *Lack of manners.*
  ☐ *Improper dress and grooming.*
  ☐ *Distracting music or surroundings.*
  ☐ *Bringing up unpleasant subjects.*

- *What things do you look forward to sharing with your wife?*

  ☐ *Events of the day.*
  ☐ *Needs and activities of the children.*
  ☐ *Ideas on home improvements.*
  ☐ *Enjoyable past memories.*
  ☐ *Spiritual lessons and insights.*
  ☐ *Clothes she is making or buying.*
  ☐ *How she really feels about certain things.*

Most wives have deep fears and emotions which they have never shared with their hubands. There are several reasons why wives do not share all of their emotions:

1. Feeling guilty for having them
2. Hoping they will pass
3. Fearing rejection from you
4. Desiring to reduce your burdens
5. Knowing you don't have answers

Your wife finds out how you will respond to her fears and whether or not you have answers by telling you about "another woman" who has the same problem. She then watches to see if you have compassion, understanding, patience, and practical help.

The fears of your wife are a test of your love because "perfect love casteth out fear" (I John 4:18). It is your responsibility to lovingly and patiently assist your wife to identify and verbalize her fears and to gain wisdom from God in resolving them.

- **What steps can you take to remove your wife's fears?**

    1. *Become aware of the fears which your wife may have:*
        - ☐ *Insecurity if you die.*
        - ☐ *Growing old.*
        - ☐ *Becoming unattractive to you.*
        - ☐ *Ill health due to past sins.*
        - ☐ *Failing as a wife or mother.*
        - ☐ *The loss of your job.*
        - ☐ *Having a mental breakdown.*
        - ☐ *Social awkwardness.*
        - ☐ *Educational deficiency.*
        - ☐ *Physical safety when alone.*
        - ☐ *Future of the children.*
        - ☐ *Being displaced by another.*

    2. *During times of intimate conversation, choose one of the above areas and ask her how she really feels about it. After her first answer, ask, "In addition to that, do you have any other feelings about it?"*

    3. *Take each fear your wife expresses and ask God for wisdom in resolving it:*
        - *What Scripture deals with that fear? Study and memorize it.*
        - *What steps of action can you take? Begin taking them.*
        - *What steps of action can she take? Encourage her to take them.*

VI. SHE NEEDS TO KNOW THAT YOU ARE AWARE OF HER PRESENCE EVEN WHEN YOUR MIND IS ON OTHER MATTERS

Your awareness of your wife's presence is her assurance of your love and protection. It was this very quality that first won your wife and assured her parents that you would be a good husband. She recalls with vivid detail your awareness of her presence and attentiveness to her needs before you were married, and she feels shut out and lonely if this is missing now.

This attentiveness to her presence is actually the true basis of manners and explains why women are so concerned about them.

Your wife has ways of "measuring" your awareness of her presence every day. This tells her how much of a part of your life she really is. Whatever manners you choose to work on must be consistently carried out. If you treat your wife like a queen one day and neglect basic manners the next day, she will feel insecure and resist your attention in order to not be hurt.

- *Love has good manners. Which of the following manners do you consistently practice?*
    - ☐ *Helping her on and off with her coat.*
    - ☐ *Seating her at the table.*
    - ☐ *Opening doors for her—especially the car door.*
    - ☐ *Lifting heavy objects for her.*
    - ☐ *Ordering for her at restaurants.*
    - ☐ *Knowing and using table manners.*
    - ☐ *Picking up after yourself at home.*
    - ☐ *Punctuality.*
    - ☐ *Properly introducing her.*
    - ☐ *Telling her your schedule.*
    - ☐ *Refraining from crude language, criticism, and improper subjects.*
    - ☐ *Personal cleanliness, neatness, and grooming.*

    Explain to your wife that you plan to work on developing good manners, and ask her to assist you by waiting for you to open the door, standing by her chair, and gently reminding you of appointments.

- *Be alert and responsive to your wife's "daily readings" of your awareness of her presence. When she asks you a question:*

  1. *Stop what you are doing.*
  2. *Look at her.*
  3. *Smile when you talk.*
  4. *Answer her question, even little questions.*
  5. *Tell her with your eyes that you love her.*

VII. SHE NEEDS TO SEE THAT YOU ARE MAKING INVESTMENTS IN HER LIFE THAT WILL EXPAND AND FULFILL HER WORLD

The major function of the head is to develop, train, and protect the rest of our body so that the whole being is able to achieve its highest and best purposes. In this same sense the husband is to be the head of the wife. (See Ephesians 5:23.)

- ☐ *Learn the spiritual gift of your wife and discern her progress in developing it, as well as the other six gifts in Romans 12.*
- ☐ *Define, with her, the responsibilities which each one has in the home.*
- ☐ *Visualize how you can add new dimensions to her responsibilities so that she can see future value to what she is presently doing.*

Answers to Quiz 4

1. False   An illegal marriage such as an incestuous one should not be rebuilt. (See Leviticus 18:1-18.) A marriage that was ended by the husband is not to be restored after the wife remarries another. (See Deuteronomy 24:1-4; Jeremiah 3:1.)

2. False   Their influence will be important, though different than it was before. Parents must continue to maintain an umbrella of protection, emotional support, wise counsel, and teaching to the grandchildren. (See Proverbs 23:22; Titus 2:3-5; Deuteronomy 4:9.)

3. False   The major cause of marital failure is the law of sin which is activated by the world, the flesh, or the devil. It must be conquered by the spiritual weapons that God has given to us. (See I Corinthians 10:13; II Corinthians 10:4-5; I John 2:15-16.)

4. False   She should first examine her own life and clear up any failure that God reveals to her. Then she must bind Satan and build a hedge of thorns around her husband. Attempting to spoil Satan's house without binding him will only result in arguments. (See Matthew 7:3-5; Mark 3:27; Ephesians 6:12.)

5. False   God has given powerful spiritual weapons to pull down Satan's strongholds and to cast down the false reasonings that have held that partner captive. (See II Corinthians 10:4-5; Hosea 2:5-7.) He also expects proper steps of appeal and correction from the partner, the parents, and the church.

6. False   The purpose of the vow is not only to establish God's marriage standards, but also to provide commitment to the marriage during times when a partner doesn't feel like being married. God holds every person responsible for his or her own words, especially vows. When either partner purposes to restore the marriage, they have a majority because God is on that partner's side. (See Matthew 12:36-37; Ecclesiastes 5:4-5; Romans 8:31-39.)

7. False   Submission to the husband should never violate God's moral laws. Sarah was praised for her submission to Abraham. Wives are instructed to follow her as long as they "do well." God expects the wife to use fervent prayer and appeal in stopping the divorce. (See I Peter 3:6; James 5:16.)

8. True   The prohibition in Deuteronomy 24:1-4 is against the wife returning to her first husband if he divorced her and she remarried someone else. It does not include the husband whose wife left him and whose wife never remarried. The possibility of return is further indicated in Malachi 2:13-16.

9. False   If an adulterous partner is unrepentant after a "hedge of thorns" has been set in place by the proper people, the offender should be warned that he or she will be turned over to God's punishment through Satan so that the lusts of the flesh shall be destroyed and that partner will repent and return to the Lord and the marriage. (See I Corinthians 11:30-33; 5:5.)

10. False   God made the husband and the wife with different responsibilities and different needs. The husband is to learn his wife's special limitations and needs and deal with her according to this knowledge. The wife is to understand her husband's needs so that she can be an effective help meet to him. (See I Peter 3:1-7; Genesis 2:18.)

Personal Commitment and Accountability

In rebuilding the marriage as far as possible:

☐ 1. I have purposed that rebuilding my marriage will be a by-product of seeking the Lord, not a goal in itself.

☐ 2. I have purposed to avoid any appearance of dating.

☐ 3. I have purposed not even to whisper any blame or accusation against my partner.

☐ 4. I have purposed to make Scriptural appeals to any steps made toward a divorce.

☐ 5. I have purposed that proper rebuilding will take time and sacrifice on my part.

☐ 6. I have purposed never to lower my standards in order to save my marriage.

☐ 7. I have purposed to protect my partner with a "hedge of thorns" on a daily basis.

☐ 8. I have purposed to follow up God's work through a "hedge of thorns."

☐ 9. I have purposed to instill God's principles in my partner by demonstrating them in my own life.

☐ 10. I have purposed to learn and meet the basic needs of my partner.

Signed _____ Date _____

REBUILDING A LEARNING RELATIONSHIP WITH YOUR CHILDREN

"Only take heed to thyself, and keep thy soul diligently, lest thou forget the things which thine eyes have seen, and lest they depart from thy heart all the days of thy life: but teach them thy sons, and thy sons' sons."

Deuteronomy 4:9

5   REBUILDER'S QUIZ

☐	☐	1. A child will probably be corrupted if allowed to live with a Godless parent or stepparent.
☐	☐	2. If a father leaves, the mother should try to fill the father's role.
☐	☐	3. A divorced father should not expect his children to listen to his counsel.
☐	☐	4. Since the sins of the parents are passed on to their children, you can expect sons and daughters to divorce if their parents were divorced.
☐	☐	5. Children should be told the causes of their parents' conflicts.
☐	☐	6. The child whose parents divorce will continue to have a damaged self-image.
☐	☐	7. With the limited time available, a parent should find out what his children enjoy doing and do it with them.
☐	☐	8. Until one party remarries, the children should be given hope that the parents can get back together again.
☐	☐	9. Children should try to avoid the questions others ask about their parents' divorce.
☐	☐	10. A father ceases to be an umbrella of protection after he leaves the family.

See answers on pages 180-182.

OF RAISING UP THE FOUNDATIONS OF MANY GODLY GENERATIONS

See the potential of investing your life into just one child.

- Your efforts to teach God's Word will last throughout all eternity, because the Word of God and the soul of your child are both eternal. (See I Peter 1:25.)
- Your child will influence the lives of many others. When God allows the loss of one or both parents, He usually has an extra special calling for the children. This was true of Joseph, Moses, Samuel, and Esther.
- The heritage that you leave in your child's life will be passed on to a multitude in just a few generations.
  If your child has four children, and each of his children have four children, this is what will happen in just four generations.

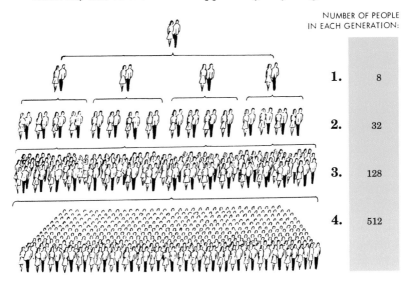

NUMBER OF PEOPLE
IN EACH GENERATION:

1.   8

2.   32

3.   128

4.   512

TOTAL   **680**

CHECK YOUR MOTIVES . . .

ON INVESTING TIME WITH YOUR CHILDREN

WRONG MOTIVES	RIGHT MOTIVES
1. To compensate for your past failures.	To obey God's command to teach your children.
2. To have a reason to keep in touch with your former partner.	To demonstrate your love and concern for your children.
3. To build your children's admiration and appreciation of you.	To build your children's admiration and appreciation for God.
4. To explain your side of the story to your children.	To teach your children to be grateful to their other parent or step-parent.
5. To learn about the problems your former partner is having.	To find ways that you can demonstrate genuine love to your former partner.
6. To teach your children your views about life.	To teach your children God's views about life.
7. To take the place of fellowship with your partner.	To rearrange priorities around God-given responsibilities.
8. To obligate your children to take care of you when you are older.	To teach your children God-given responsibilities to the whole family.
9. To prove to your friends that your children have not rejected you.	To prove to your children that you have not rejected them.

EXPECT BARRIERS . . .

TO ANY TEACHING EFFORTS BECAUSE OF PAST HURTS AND DISAPPOINTMENTS

BARRIERS	HOW TO REMOVE THEM
1. DISTRUST	Ask each child what promises you have made in the past but never fulfilled. Then set about fulfilling the ones you can, and asking for forgiveness and release on the ones you cannot.
2. DISRESPECT	Think through Scriptural ways of humbling yourself before your children, such as submitting to authority, admitting when you are wrong, and being silent when falsely accused. ". . . Before honour is humility" (Proverbs 15:33).
3. DISINTEREST	Learn how to create curiosity by being contagiously enthusiastic and by learning how to ask intriguing questions which your children will want you to answer. We are to be the salt of the earth, and one of the functions of salt is to create thirst. If you do not have any ability to create hunger and thirst for righteousness in your children, God says you are good for nothing. (See Matthew 5:13.)
4. UNAVAILABILITY	Work out an organized plan of teaching goals combined, if possible, with interesting activities. Give advance notice by making appointments. Half of the enjoyment of an event is looking forward to it.

5. BITTERNESS	Clear up past offenses toward your children by telling them how you were wrong and asking them to forgive you. Also make sure that you have cleared your conscience with your partner so that your children are not able to take up offenses.
6. INTERRUPTIONS	Be flexible in teaching your children. Learn how to use unexpected events or pressures to teach what is needed at the moment, rather than what you had planned to teach.
7. EVASIVENESS	Find the right opportunity to ask precise personal questions which would reveal hidden moral impurity; then explain the principles of moral freedom as explained in Goal Number 1, pages 9-35.
8. COMPETITION	When children feel that their parents cannot be counted on, they will tend to build their security or interests around other people or things. Until you re-earn their trust, you may have to compete with neighborhood friends, hobbies, sports, television, books, and records. Where possible, include their friends in your activities. As your children see the value of what you are teaching, and as they place more trust in you, the need for you to compete for your children's attention will greatly decrease.

4   IDENTIFY GOALS . . .

BY ASKING YOUR CHILDREN ABOUT THEIR WISHES

By asking questions and listening for answers, discover what are fears and dreams of your children. These must then be translated into basic Scriptural goals.

FEARS	BASIC GOALS
1. Fear of rejection	To learn how to have self-acceptance.
2. Fear of ridicule	To learn how to stand alone.
3. Fear of loneliness	To learn how to be content in the Lord and how to make good friends.
4. Fear of competition	To learn skills and how to praise others who win.
5. Fear of habits	To learn how to overcome habits.
6. Fear of death	To learn how to set affections on things above.
7. Fear of want	To learn how to give to God and see Him meet needs in answer to prayer.
8. Fear of the unknown	To learn how God provides and protects.

ORGANIZE CONTENT . . .   **5**

AROUND TWENTY OBJECTIVES TO BE REACHED

- ☐ Show each child how to be sure about his or her salvation.
- ☐ Encourage each child to dedicate his or her life to God's will.
- ☐ Help each child to come to self-acceptance.
- ☐ Guide each child to get under the protection of authority.
- ☐ Work with each child to gain a clear conscience.
- ☐ Explain to each child how to have a forgiving spirit.
- ☐ Demonstrate to each child how to respond to irritations.
- ☐ Establish accountability with each child to engraft the Word and use it to conquer moral impurity.
- ☐ Instruct each child on how to meditate.
- ☐ Help each child learn how to witness to his or her friends.
- ☐ Set up with each child a daily Bible reading program.
- ☐ Provide for each child challenging biographies of great Christians.
- ☐ Discuss with each child God's standards for dating.
- ☐ Work with each child on learning and applying principles of finances.
- ☐ Help each child to establish an effective prayer life.
- ☐ Train each child how to make right friends and avoid wrong ones.
- ☐ Challenge each child to stand alone against evil.
- ☐ Assist each child to discover and develop his spiritual gift.
- ☐ Show each child how to become an active church member.
- ☐ Help each child to visualize a spiritual purpose in life.

NOTE: Each of these goals is presented in the Basic Seminar.

ESTABLISH ACCOUNTABILITY... 6

IN FOLLOWING THROUGH ON THESE GOALS

The most effective basis of any teaching relationship is accountability for progress. Without this mutual agreement to check up on each other and share victories and defeats, the teaching process will either bog down and soon cease, or it will not produce the expected results in daily living.

Accountability involves understood goals and agreed-upon questions. Here are some examples of questions for accountability. Encourage your children to ask you these questions; also request their permission for you to ask them the same questions.

1. What did you learn from your Bible reading this morning?

2. What Scripture did you meditate on as you went to sleep last night?

3. What Scripture are you memorizing?

4. Is there anyone you need to ask forgiveness from, or is there anyone that you need to forgive?

5. What opportunities have you had this week to stand alone?

6. Were you able to successfully resist the last temptation you experienced?

7. Are you having consistent victory in your thought life?

8. Which friends are you wanting to lead to Christ?

9. What plans have you committed yourself to in the next few weeks?

10. What prayers have you seen God answer in the last week?

CONCENTRATE ON CHARACTER . . .

AS YOU RESPOND TO LIFE SITUATIONS TOGETHER

The most effective setting for teaching is not the formal classroom but the unexpected situations that you face every day. If you are familiar with the following character qualities, you will be able to teach them to your children, even through the difficult situations and circumstances of your rebuilding program.

QUALITY	OPERATIONAL DEFINITIONS
1. ALERTNESS *vs.* *Unawareness*	Being aware of the physical and spiritual events taking place around me so that I can have the right responses to them. (See Mark 14:38.)
2. ATTENTIVENESS *vs.* *Unconcern*	Showing the worth of a person by giving undivided attention to his words and emotions. (See Hebrews 2:1.)
3. AVAILABILITY *vs.* *Self-centeredness*	Adjusting my personal responsibilities around the needs of those whom I am serving. (See Philippians 2:20-21.)
4. BOLDNESS *vs.* *Fearfulness*	Confidence that what I have to say or do is true and right and just in the sight of God. (See Acts 4:29.)
5. CAUTIOUSNESS *vs.* *Rashness*	Knowing how important right timing is in accomplishing right actions. (See Proverbs 19:2.)

6. COMPASSION
vs.
Indifference

Investing whatever is necessary to heal the hurts of others. (See I John 3:17.)

7. CONTENTMENT
vs.
Covetousness

Realizing God has provided everything I need for my present happiness. (See I Timothy 6:8.)

8. CREATIVITY
vs.
Under-achievement

Applying God's wisdom and practical insights to a need or task. (See Romans 12:2.)

9. DECISIVENESS
vs.
Double-mindedness

The ability to finalize difficult decisions based on the will and ways of God. (See James 1:5.)

10. DEFERENCE
vs.
Rudeness

Limiting my freedom to speak and act in order not to offend the tastes of others. (See Romans 14:21.)

11. DEPENDABILITY
vs.
Inconsistency

Fulfilling what I consented to do even if it means unexpected sacrifice. (See Psalm 15:4.)

12. DETERMINATION
vs.
Faint-heartedness

Purposing to accomplish God's goals in God's time regardless of the opposition. (See II Timothy 4:7-8.)

13. DILIGENCE
vs.
Slothfulness

Visualizing each task as a special assignment from the Lord and using all my energies to accomplish it. (See Colossians 3:23.)

14. DISCERNMENT
vs.
Judgment

The God-given ability to understand why things happen to others and to me. (See I Samuel 16:7.)

15. DISCRETION
vs.
Simple-mindedness

The ability to avoid words, actions, and attitudes which could result in undesirable consequences. (See Proverbs 22:3.)

16. ENDURANCE
vs.
Giving up

The inward strength to withstand stress to accomplish God's best. (See Galatians 6:9.)

QUALITY	OPERATIONAL DEFINITIONS
17. ENTHUSIASM *vs.* *Apathy*	Expressing with my spirit the joy of my soul. (See I Thessalonians 5:16-19.)
18. FAITH *vs.* *Presumption*	Visualizing what God intends to do in a given situation and acting in harmony with it. (See Hebrews 11:1.)
19. FLEXIBILITY *vs.* *Resistance*	Not setting my affections on ideas or plans which could be changed by God or others. (See Colossians 3:2.)
20. FORGIVENESS *vs.* *Rejection*	Clearing the record of those who have wronged me and allowing God to love them through me. (See Ephesians 4:32.)
21. GENEROSITY *vs.* *Stinginess*	Realizing that all I have belongs to God and using it for His purposes. (See II Corinthians 9:6.)
22. GENTLENESS *vs.* *Harshness*	Showing personal care and concern in meeting the needs of others. (See I Thessalonians 2:7.)
23. GRATEFULNESS *vs.* *Unthankfulness*	Making known to God and others in what ways they have benefited my life. (See I Corinthians 4:7.)
24. HOSPITALITY *vs.* *Loneliness*	Cheerfully sharing food, shelter, and spiritual refreshment with those whom God brings into my life. (See Hebrews 13:2.)
25. HUMILITY *vs.* *Pride*	Seeing the contrast between God's holiness and my sinfulness. (See James 4:6.)
26. INITIATIVE *vs.* *Unresponsiveness*	Recognizing and doing what needs to be done before I am asked to do it. (See Romans 12:21.)

27. JOYFULNESS *vs.* *Self-pity*	The result of knowing that God is perfecting His life in others through me. (See Proverbs 15:13.)
28. JUSTICE *vs.* *Fairness*	Personal responsibility to God's unchanging laws. (See Micah 6:8.)
29. LOVE *vs.* *Selfishness*	Giving to others' basic needs without having personal reward as my motive. (See I Corinthians 13:3.)
30. LOYALTY *vs.* *Unfaithfulness*	Using difficult times to demonstrate my commitment to God and to those whom He has called me to serve. (See John 15:13.)
31. MEEKNESS *vs.* *Anger*	Yielding my personal rights and expectations to God. (See Psalm 62:5.)
32. OBEDIENCE *vs.* *Willfulness*	Fulfilling instructions so that God and the one I am serving will be fully satisfied. (See II Corinthians 10:5.)
33. ORDERLINESS *vs.* *Disorganization*	Arranging my life and surroundings so that God has maximum freedom to achieve His goals through me. (See I Corinthians 14:40.)
34. PATIENCE *vs.* *Restlessness*	Accepting a difficult situation from God without giving Him a deadline to remove it. (See Romans 5:3-4.)
35. PERSUASIVENESS *vs.* *Contentiousness*	Using words which cause the listener's spirit to confirm that he is hearing truth. (See II Timothy 2:24.)
36. PUNCTUALITY *vs.* *Tardiness*	Showing respect for other people and the limited time that God has given to them. (See Ecclesiastes 3:1.)
37. RESOURCEFUL- NESS *vs.* *Wastefulness*	Wise use of that which others would normally overlook or discard. (See Luke 16:10.)

QUALITY	OPERATIONAL DEFINITIONS
38. RESPONSIBILITY *vs.* *Unreliability*	Knowing and doing what both God and others are expecting from me. (See Romans 14:12.)
39. REVERENCE *vs.* *Disrespect*	Awareness of how God is working through the people and events in my life to produce the character of Christ in me. (See Proverbs 23:17-18.)
40. SECURITY *vs.* *Anxiety*	Structuring my life around what is eternal and cannot be destroyed or taken away. (See John 6:27.)
41. SELF-CONTROL *vs.* *Self-indulgence*	Instant obedience to the initial promptings of God's Spirit. (See Galatians 5:24-25.)
42. SENSITIVITY *vs.* *Callousness*	Knowing by the prompting of God's Spirit what words and actions will benefit the lives of others. (See Romans 12:15.)
43. SINCERITY *vs.* *Hypocrisy*	Eagerness to do what is right with transparent motives. (See I Peter 1:22.)
44. THRIFTINESS *vs.* *Extravagance*	Not letting myself or others spend that which is not necessary. (See Luke 16:11.)
45. THOROUGHNESS *vs.* *Incompleteness*	Realizing that each of our tasks will be reviewed and rewarded by God. (See Proverbs 18:15.)
46. TOLERANCE *vs.* *Prejudice*	Viewing every person as a valuable individual whom God created and loves. (See Philippians 2:2.)

| 47. TRUTHFULNESS | Earning future trust by accurately report- |
| *vs.* *Deception* | ing past facts. (See Ephesians 4:25.) |

47. **TRUTHFULNESS**
    vs.
    Deception

Earning future trust by accurately reporting past facts. (See Ephesians 4:25.)

48. **WISDOM**
    vs.
    Natural Inclinations

Seeing and responding to life situations from God's frame of reference. (See Proverbs 9:10.)

49. **VIRTUE**
    vs.
    Impurity

The influence God is having on others through my life regardless of my past failures. (See II Peter 1:3.)

THE HIDDEN COST OF CHARACTER TRAINING

A nine-year-old boy sat in church listening to the soloist. As she sang the word "anxiety," he quietly leaned over to his mother and said, "Mom, anxiety is the opposite of security."

On another occasion this nine-year-old boy walked home from school and said to his parents, "Today I had a chance to use loyalty." Then he explained how. He had asked one of his classmates to get something for him. As a result, that classmate got into trouble because he was out of his seat. This boy went up to the teacher and explained that it was his fault and asked to have his name put on the board instead of his friend's name.

Another time this boy said to his parents, "I have been thinking about meekness all day long." When asked why, he said, "It seemed like everything was making me mad today."

School was not easy for him. In fact, he failed the first grade. Then he started memorizing Scripture and his grades dramatically improved. Whenever his grades started slipping, he knew it was because he had not been as faithful as he should have been in the Word.

The principle of "active duty"

No doubt every parent would be thrilled to have sons and daughters exhibiting such an understanding of character. It is true that the parents were using the Character Clues Game and the *Character Sketches* book with him, but the real understanding came when that son observed his parents demonstrating the true meaning of the qualities they were teaching him. Some of these are described in the following account:

"Both my husband and I were deeply influenced at the Basic Seminar, but the big change occurred after my husband attended the Advanced Seminar in 1974. He grasped the concept of being an active member of the Lord's army. The disciplines that followed tested my submissiveness and willingness to trust him to be our spiritual leader.

The surrender that leads to freedom

"My husband had a good teaching position and I was an operating room registered nurse—a job I loved even more than being the creative homemaker God intended me to be. In spite of this, we were $10,000.00 in debt. My husband asked me to quit my job, and I did.

"Next, we sold our brand new four-bedroom house and moved into a two-bedroom apartment! An even bigger adjustment was moving from Los Angeles to a farm in Texas. What a change—from the prestige and excitement of working in a hospital operating room to the privilege of hoeing in a cotton field during the summer. At times I felt that the Lord had completely forgotten about me, but I soon learned that the wisdom of the Lord is so much bigger than my tiny frame of reference.

The reorganization of priorities

"It was during the following three years that my husband and I really began to establish our goals and sincerely apply the teachings of the Seminar to our lives. We had a time to memorize and meditate on God's Word. We also had the privilege of really experiencing God's grace because we were humbled, and humbled, and humbled some more.

"My husband worked for his father as a hired hand. When things looked bleak, he continued to be faithful in claiming God's promises for us. His desire was for us to get our home in order and then reach out to others. It would have been so much easier to reach out to others than to go through the painful process of getting our home in order.

"On the farm our salary is much smaller than we had been used to, but now we are almost entirely out of debt. From the world's eyes it seemed impossible, and many times I thought, 'If only my husband would let me work, we could get out of debt much faster.' Now I praise the Lord that I did not work because during this time God illustrated His power through miraculous answers to prayer for the things we needed. Among them was a car and a sewing machine.

The training that goes against natural inclinations

"I couldn't sew when I got the machine, but the Lord has been giving me the patience to learn; and I have made all my clothes and even the curtains for our home. It has been fun and fulfilling. We are getting rid of the things that we feel we can do without, such as the television set. My husband is helping me simplify my life and I appreciate what he is doing. I am now working on becoming the woman the Lord talks about in Proverbs 31. So much of her character goes against my natural inclinations.

"My learning will continue, but meanwhile I never could have imagined the results of these last three years. My husband and I enjoy a growing oneness of spirit. Our son is reflecting the character which we are learning. We are achieving financial freedom, and through the changes in our lives our relatives have wanted to attend a Seminar.

"My father was led to salvation when he did attend, plus my brother-in-law. The Seminar ministry also caused other members of my family to rededicate their lives. Before my brothers would set their wedding dates, they made sure their future brides attended a Seminar.

"The spiritual revival in my immediate family is unbelievable. It makes any price we paid seem like a very small investment."

Used by permission of each member of the family.

LEARNING RESOURCES . . .

To assist you in building Scriptural principles, convictions, character, and standards in your life and in the lives of your children.

1. Establish a program of answering your children's questions. Make it a "game" at bedtime, and most children will love it. Tell them, "We are going to play 'The Answer Game.' You have all day to think of one question that you want to ask. It can be a question about God, the Bible, my work, our family, my background, or things that have happened to you. Before you go to sleep, I will come to your room and give you the best, most honest answer that I can. If I do not know the answer, I will do all that I can to find the answer."

2. Set up individual appointments and dates with your sons and daughters to do things together. Dress appropriately for the occasion. Relax and be yourself. Be a good listener. Give your full concentration to each one personally, as a father is instructed to do in I Thessalonians 2:11-12.

3. Begin a "life notebook" with each child. A life notebook is a place to record insights, experiences, and lessons learned from Scripture and from life. Add to it from time to time as your child expresses an interest, but do not force your child to contribute to the notebook. Even an untouched life notebook on the shelf can be motivation for learning.

4. Encourage your children to show you when you exhibit the negative character traits of anger, impatience, deception, or ungratefulness, and thank them when they do so. Tell them how you are going to ask forgiveness of those whom you have wronged, and share with them the results when you have done so.

5. Design achievable memorization goals. Give prizes when these goals are completed, and teach your children how to meditate on those verses as they go to sleep at night and as they wake up in the morning.

MEN'S MANUAL

CHARACTER SKETCHES

LIFE NOTEBOOK

CHARACTER CLUES

COMMANDS OF CHRIST

PINEAPPLE STORY

EAGLE STORY

Answers to Quiz 5

1. False   If the other parent instills the principles of God's Word in his life and is a living demonstration of them, the child will be able to see a contrast between righteous living and Godless living. Moses becomes a reassuring testimony of what can take place when such a contrast exists. He saw first hand that the pleasures of sin lasted only for a season; therefore, he chose righteousness even though it meant suffering. (See Hebrews 11:24-26.) Samuel was also exposed to wickedness when he was growing up with Eli's two sons. (See I Samuel 2:12-17.)

2. False   The mother should make it clear to her children that she is their mother, not their father. She should explain that God is their father and that He will constantly watch, protect, and chasten them. (See Psalm 68:5.) Christ's earthly father died during His youth. His focus throughout life, however, was on His Heavenly Father. (See Luke 2:49.)

3. True   Children should listen to the counsel of parents even if they are divorced. However, the father who is out of the house should not demand a hearing; instead, he should earn it. This is the basis of a meek spirit which God requires. (See Psalm 29:9; II Timothy 2:24-25; I Peter 3:15.)

4. False   God does state that the sins of the parents are passed on to the third and fourth generation. However, He also promises that He shows mercy to thousands who love Him and keep His commandments. Children at any level can break the chain of their forefathers' sins, especially as they learn how to enter into Christ's resurrection power. (See Exodus 20:5-6; II Corinthians 5:17.)

5. True   The root causes of parents' failures should be discreetly shared with the children so the children can prepare for those weaknesses in their own makeups. Root causes such as pride, lack of self-control, and greed may find different manifestations in children, so it is not necessary for detailed descriptions of the manifestations in parents. Nor should failures by shared to accuse another parent or gain the children's support. Scripture teaches the importance of acknowledging the sins of the parents. (See Ephesians 5:12; Jeremiah 14:20.)

6. False   This can be true, but it doesn't need to be if either parent teaches the child Scriptural principles of self-acceptance. Every person has personal and family scars and defects. Children can turn these into marks of God's ownership, motivations for character development, and means of becoming more like Christ. He had the stigma of an "illegitimate" birth. (See Philippians 2:13; Galatians 6:17; John 8:41.)

7. False   With limited time a parent should carefully plan how to most effectively teach the principles of God's Word. If these times can be combined with enjoyable activities, all the better. However, the role of a parent is to train the child, not to entertain the child. (See Deuteronomy 7:9; Proverbs 22:6.)

8. False   The hope should not be in the parents, but in the Lord's larger purposes, whether the marriage succeeds or fails. Hope deferred makes the heart sick. It also can cause children to become bitter toward parents and toward God. Instead, the children should commit their parents' marriage to the Lord, and concentrate on what God is wanting to teach them through this experience. Vital character qualities can be deeply learned during this time, especially the quality of patience, which is "accepting a difficult situation from God without giving Him a deadline to remove it." (See Proverbs 13:12, 3:5–6; Romans 5:1–5.)

9. False   Instead of avoiding questions, children should be taught how to give a clear, concise statement which does not blame either parent or reflect any trace of bitterness. "The heart of the righteous studieth to answer . . ." (Proverbs 15:28). It would be very encouraging for children to be able to say, "The marriage of my parents failed, but now we are learning how to be rebuilders." (See I Peter 3:15; Proverbs 15:23.)

10. False   The father will provide spiritual protection; however, he will not be the primary umbrella of protection. The remaining parent will have the legal authority and responsibility. However, the father continues to have Scriptural responsibilities to the children. Part of that responsibility involves fervent prayer for protection. (See Malachi 4:6; I Samuel 12:23.)

Personal Commitment and Accountability

In rebuilding a learning relationship with the children:

☐ 1. I purpose to rearrange my priorities around the learning needs of my children.

☐ 2. I am committed to a lifelong training program for the purpose of raising up the foundations of many Godly generations.

☐ 3. I purpose to have the right motives for investing time with my children.

☐ 4. I am prepared to respond wisely to barriers to learning.

☐ 5. I purpose to identify the fears and wishes of my children and translate them into Godly goals for their lives.

☐ 6. I purpose to establish a continuing program of accountability with my children in order to maintain spiritual growth.

☐ 7. I am committed to building character qualities in my life and instilling them in the lives of my children.

☐ 8. I purpose to be alert to other resources which will assist my children in becoming mighty in spirit.

Signed _____ Date _____

GOAL NUMBER **6**

REBUILDING PAST FAILURES INTO A NEW LIFE MESSAGE

"Blessed be . . . the God of all comfort; Who comforteth us in all our tribulation, that we may be able to comfort them which are in any trouble, by the comfort wherewith we ourselves are comforted of God."

II Corinthians 1:3-4

6 REBUILDER'S QUIZ

Match each
"message"
to the right
person:

The most important messages of the Bible have grown out of the failure in the lives of God's people.

Can you identify these people?

☐

Adam
(Genesis 3)

1. "Twice I was in danger of losing my partner. Each time I tried to keep my partner by lies and deception. God reproved me for this, and taught me how to keep a loved one by fully yielding that loved one to Him."

☐

Rachel
(Genesis 29-35)

2. "I was faced with the situation of being separated from my partner or lowering my standards. I willfully and wrongfully chose to lower my standards. The consequences of my failure are still being felt. I confessed my sin. God forgave me and gave me an important message for my children."

☐

Eve
(Genesis 3)

3. "One evening when I should have been working, I was relaxing. I fell into temptation and committed adultery. People greatly respected me, so I tried to cover my sin. This resulted in greater sin. God publicly exposed all my sin, and taught me the true meaning of repentance and fearing the Lord. I have written out my testimony for others."

☐

Abraham
(Genesis 12-22)

4. "I spent many years trying to keep the law of God. The problem was that I was trying to do it in my own energy. As a result, I failed. I failed so badly that I became an accomplice to a murder! But God forgave me and taught me how to keep His law by His power rather than mine. I have been able to teach many others this same truth."

5. "I wanted to please my husband. He wanted something that I could not give to him. I should have just trusted God to work it out, but instead I took matters into my own hands. My efforts caused conflicts from the very beginning; and they continue to do so, but God is faithful. He finally taught me the secret of trusting Him and obeying my husband. This secret can help other women if they follow it."

Isaac
(Genesis 26)

6. "God states that the sins of the parents are visited to their children. I can testify to this accuracy. The very same problems that my parents had during their marriage I had in mine. I should have learned from their mistakes, but I didn't. God was merciful to me when I returned to Him."

Sarah
(Genesis 16)

7. "There were many valid reasons why I could not trust my husband. Others couldn't trust him either! As a result, we didn't have the closeness that we should have had in our marriage. This caused severe conflicts among our children. Eventually, my husband totally conquered his problem and became an example to many. Both I and most of the children got out from under his authority and were severely judged by God."

Paul
(Acts 22)

8. "There is no excuse for my failure. I had the perfect husband, no competition from other women, an ideal environment, no financial worries, and a very close fellowship with the Lord. You would have thought that I had no complaints, however, my message to other women is that no matter how much we have, Satan can still defeat us if we listen to him at all."

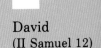

David
(II Samuel 12)

See answers on page 208.

1   WHAT IS A LIFE MESSAGE?

A "life message" is a continuing explanation of how God is working through our human weaknesses to show the riches of His grace and the exceeding greatness of His power. (See II Corinthians 4:7-12.)

WHO SHOULD DEVELOP A LIFE MESSAGE?

Every Christian should concentrate on developing an effective life message. God has called every one of us to be a witness. "But ye shall receive power, after that the Holy Ghost is come upon you: and ye shall be witnesses unto me . . ." (Acts 1:8).

A witness is a person who tells what he has personally seen and heard. "That which we have seen and heard declare we unto you . . ." (I John 1:3).

HOW CAN A LIFE MESSAGE BE DEVELOPED?

We can develop a life message by writing down our experiences and the truths which God is teaching us through them. This is essential if we are going to accurately report to others what God has done in our lives.

The theme of every effective life message must be faith. We grow from faith to faith. (See Romans 1:17.) "But without faith it is impossible to please him . . ." (Hebrews 11:6). Every great biography in Scripture illustrates the faith of men and women acting upon God's Word. (See Hebrews 11.)

Each step of faith is difficult because it requires death to self and human reasoning. However, the results of obedience are exciting and challenging to others and bring glory to God.

Chapter 1—How I became a Christian

- Faith in God's provision of salvation. ". . . Giving all diligence, add to your faith . . ." (II Peter 1:5).

Chapter 2—How I made changes in my life so that I could be a more effective influence for Godliness

- Faith in the standards of righteousness which God has established.

- The influence that we have on the lives of others through moral excellence. ". . . Add to your faith virtue . . ." (II Peter 1:5).

Chapter 3—How I totally dedicated my life to God's will

- Faith in the principles of God's Word. ". . . And [add] to virtue knowledge" (II Peter 1:5.)

- Dedication: As an act of worship. (See Romans 12:1-2.)

Chapter 4—How I became active in serving the Lord

- Faith in the disciplines that God requires for fruitful service. "And to knowledge [add] temperance [self-control] . . ." (II Peter 1:6).

- Christian service as a by-product of a disciplined life.

Chapter 5—How I was misunderstood and rejected in my attempts to serve others

- Faith in the protection of God in the midst of suffering. "... And to temperance [self-control] [add] patience ..." (II Peter 1:6).

- Patience and endurance during times of predicted suffering. "Beloved, think it not strange concerning the fiery trial which is to try you, as though some strange thing happened unto you" (I Peter 4:12).

Chapter 6—How I learned to be more like Christ through suffering

- Faith in the comfort and insights in Scripture during and after suffering. "... And [add] to patience godliness" (II Peter 1:6).

- Godliness: Becoming like Christ in our attitudes and responses to those who hurt us.

Chapter 7—How I have been able to share with others in similar troubles the same truths God has taught me

- Faith in the effectiveness of God's comfort and counsel to others.
  "And to godliness [add] brotherly kindness ..." (II Peter 1:7).

Chapter 8—How God allowed me to reproduce the spiritual maturity of my life in the lives of others

- Faith in the command to demonstrate genuine love. "... And to brotherly kindness [add] charity [love]" (II Peter 1:7).

FIVE BASIC PARTS OF AN EFFECTIVE CHAPTER IN YOUR LIFE MESSAGE

3

The contents of each chapter within your life message should contain the following five parts:

PART ONE—The Failure

Wrong responses to the trials, challenges, needs, heartaches, and weaknesses which came into my life. (My children began to rebel against me and my spouse threatened to divorce me.)

PART TWO—My Efforts

The human solutions which I tried to use in solving the problems which came into my life. (I became more involved in my business and avoided contact with my wife and children.)

PART THREE—The Consequences

The cause-and-effect results which took place when I attempted to solve my problems with human reasoning and self-effort. (Conditions got worse in my family and in my business. I became totally discouraged and gave up.)

PART FOUR—Applying God's Truth

The discovery of God's principles and the application of them to the problems I was having. (After learning how I had really hurt my wife and children, I asked their forgiveness and rearranged my priorities around their needs.)

PART FIVE—The Results

The rewards of applying God's principles to my problems. (God has restored my marriage, my children have come under my authority, and God has greatly prospered my business.)

THE FIVE PARTS OF A LIFE MESSAGE FROM SCRIPTURE

The following outline summarizes a biography in the Scriptures, and it clearly illustrates the effectiveness of the five parts of a life message.

PART ONE—The Failure

One evening, while taking a walk, I saw a beautiful woman. We met secretly, and that night I committed adultery with her. Later she told me that she was pregnant.

PART TWO—My Efforts

I tried to encourage this woman's husband to have a physical relationship with her so that he would believe the child was his. When that didn't work, I arranged to have him killed. Then I married the woman.

PART THREE —The Consequences

God publicly exposed my sin. The child that was born became sick and died, and my failure resulted in continual conflicts within my family. Eventually, four of my other sons were killed; and worst of all, the heathen were allowed to blaspheme God.

PART FOUR—Applying God's Truth

When God convicted me of my sin, I confessed it to Him. I repented before the Lord, I mourned for the child, and I asked God to give me His mercy.

PART FIVE—The Results

God was gracious to me. He forgave me and cleansed me. He restored unto me the joy of His salvation; and He allowed me to strengthen the lives of many others by the Psalms which I wrote as the result of my failure, especially Psalm 51. (Based on II Samuel 11-19.)

THE NEGLECTED TRUTH
OF MOST LIFE MESSAGES

We always like to hear a story that has a happy ending. The biographies that God has given to us in Scripture, however, do not always fit that unrealistic form. The power of God's messages comes from the *continuing limitations* which result from failures.

These physical limitations provide powerful motivation for your listeners: If they will learn the lessons that God has taught you, they will not have to suffer the same physical limitations in their lives.

> *For example . . .*
>
> *If a man is careless while mowing his lawn and puts his fingers under the whirling blade, they will be chopped off. He will certainly repent of his carelessness and purpose not to do it again. However, the fingers will still be missing. This physical limitation will be a continuing reminder to him, and a vivid warning to others, not to be careless. If the man were to conceal his mutilated hand with a glove, the real impact of the warning would be lost; but by turning the loss of his fingers into a useful and continuous message to others, this man's carelessness takes on redemptive value. The more important the message, the more inward joy he can experience.*

This is God's way to forgive sin. He puts it out of His sight, but in order to build Christ's character in us and to give clear warnings to others, He allows continuing physical limitations. If we respond to them wisely and obediently, they will actually increase our inward beauty, and the glory of Christ will shine more brightly as we become living witnesses of His truth.

GOD'S EXAMPLES OF CONTINUING LIMITATIONS

God records the failures of men and women in Scripture as a part of their life messages to us. (See Romans 15:4.)	When they failed, God put a restriction on them which affected their further service.

FAILURES	LIMITATIONS FROM FAILURES
ADAM Ate forbidden fruit (See Genesis 3:6.)	Ground cursed "For your sake" (See Genesis 3:17.)
EVE Ate forbidden fruit (See Genesis 3:6.)	New pressures of submission to husband (See Genesis 3:16; I Peter 3:1.)
PAUL Persecuted and imprisoned Christians (See Acts 22:4.)	Called to suffer (See Acts 9:16.)
DAVID Committed adultery and murder (See II Samuel 11.)	Continual warfare (See II Samuel 12:10.)
PRODIGAL SON Lived with harlots (See Luke 15:30.)	Loss of inheritance All belonged to brother
CORINTHIAN CHRISTIAN Committed immorality (See I Corinthians 5:1.)	Expelled from church until repentant (See II Corinthians 2:6-11.)

To make sure that they did not forget the lessons which they had learned, God gave them a reminder of the past.	Each limitation had a precise benefit for them and instruction for us. (See I Corinthians 10:11.)
REMINDERS OF LIMITATIONS	**BENEFIT OF LIMITATIONS**
Sweat, sorrow thistles and thorns (See Genesis 3:17-19.)	Greater dependence on God for daily food and health (See Matthew 6:11.)
Pain, sorrow related to childbirth Desire to control husband (See Genesis 3:16.)	Protection under the headship of the husband and Christ (See I Corinthians 11:3.)
Prison chains Thorn in flesh for revelations (See II Corinthians 12:7.)	Removal of pride and furtherance of the Gospel (See II Corinthians 12:7; Philippians 1:12.)
Loss of child Family problems (See II Samuel 12:11, 15.) Memories (See Psalm 51:3.)	Motivation to daily communication with God (See Psalms.)
Becomes a servant under the discipline of older brother when father dies (See Luke 15:19, 31.)	Ability to learn greatness through serving (See Matthew 23:11-12.)
Destruction of fleshly desires (See I Corinthians 5:5.)	Salvation of the spirit in the day of Christ (See I Corinthians 5:5.)

THE WISDOM OF GOD'S LIMITATION ON A REMARRIED PERSON

God has established several requirements for those who hold the church offices of bishop or deacon. One of those requirements is that they must be the husband of one wife. (See I Timothy 3:2, 12.)

This requirement, therefore, becomes a limitation to those who are divorced and remarried. The limitation does not involve other types of Christian service. It is confined to elected church officers. (The only other application is in regard to the qualification of widows, in I Timothy 5:3-16.)

People can respond in two ways to this Scriptural limitation. Either they can interpret it in an attempt to explain it away; or they can use the same study and creativity to discern why God has given such a restriction.

Here are three important reasons for this restriction:

1. It protects church discipline

The vital responsibility of disciplining the members of the local church rests in the hands of bishops and deacons or, in other words, the elected church officials. The personal lives of those who discipline must be free from blame. If a church leader's authority can be questioned as a result of his violating God's marriage standards, his decisions in church discipline will certainly be affected. He will tend to be either too lenient or too harsh. (For further study on this subject, see Chapter 2.)

2. It avoids hurtful tensions and criticism

If a divorced and remarried person is allowed to hold an elected office in a church, those members of the church who strongly believe in the Scriptural requirements for church officers are going to feel disappointed and angry. They will then be accused of being harsh, unloving, unforgiving, and legalistic by those who take a more casual approach to the Scriptural requirements for church leadership. The result of this conflict will be bitterness, tension, and a lack of unity in the church.

3. It gives the divorced and remarried person the freedom to develop a servant's heart

When others realize that there are continuing limitations which result from a remarriage, they will be challenged and warned to strengthen and protect their own marriages. Young people especially will be motivated to seek God's will in their marriage decisions.

FAILURE	LIMITATION	REMINDER	BENEFITS
DIVORCED PERSON WHO HAS RE-MARRIED Violated marriage vow and symbolism of the marriage relationship. *(See Ephesians 5:21-33.)*	Excluded from offices of Bishop and Deacon *(See I Timothy 3:2, 12.)* Excluded from "Widows' list" *(See I Timothy 5:9.)*	Personal failures and reproach which can be turned into a meaningful "life message" "Beauty for ashes" *(See Isaiah 61:1-4.) (See Proverbs 6:33.)*	Motivation to others to maintain marriage standards Freedom to be an example as a servant and to avoid the pressures that are experienced by the elected church leaders *(See James 3:1.)*

HOW TO TRANSFORM PAINFUL MEMORIES INTO AN EFFECTIVE LIFE MESSAGE

Satan will try to cause us to regret our past sins, but God will give us the power to overcome the continuing condemnation of past failures. (See II Corinthians 7:10.)

Satan wants us to say, "I don't know why I've failed. I'm not really a bad person." God wants us to say, "What I did only confirms God's evaluation of how wicked and deceitful my heart is." (See Jeremiah 17:9.)

Satan will urge us to remember our failures with the words, "If only I had not . . . ." This "circle of regret" will only lead to physical, emotional, or mental breakdowns.

Transforming painful memories by filling our minds with truth

When we accept the full responsibility for our failures, receive God's cleansing through the blood of Christ, and dedicate our lives to God's will, we can fill our minds with the following truths.

1. What I did was totally wrong. I am guilty and worthy of God's just punishment.

2. Because God is just, my sin must be punished. For this purpose God sentenced His own Son to die.

6. Every time I recall my failure and appropriately share it with others, it makes me realize how much I owe to God.

3. Therefore it was my sin that nailed Jesus to the cross. "He was wounded for my transgressions . . ."

5. I am also redeemed by His blood. Thus, I belong to Him. I am no longer my own. I am His "bond servant."

4. When I receive Christ's payment for my sin, I don't have to pay the penalty for it. I am cleansed by the blood of Christ.

NO MATTER HOW GREAT YOUR FAILURE . . .

YOU CAN HAVE AN EFFECTIVE LIFE MESSAGE

Paul confessed that he was the greatest sinner who ever lived. (See I Timothy 1:15.) This was not false humility on Paul's part—it was true.

There was a reason why God chose to make the "chief of sinners" into the greatest messenger of truth that the Church has ever seen. The reason is that God does not want anyone in the world to ever think that he or she is too sinful to be saved or too wicked to have an effective ministry.

After Paul became a Christian, he could have lived with a cycle of regret. He could have dealt with all of his shameful memories with the repeated thought, "If only I had not done them."

One memory that was particularly painful for Paul was the assistance which he gave in the killing of the Godly church leader, Stephen. (See Acts 7.) He could have condemned himself as a murderer, since he was an accomplice to the crime. (See Acts 22:20.)

His cycle of regret would have been as follows:

4. If only Stephen had not been killed.

1. If only I was not there when Stephen was stoned.

3. If only I had not held the garments of those who stoned Stephen. (See Acts 22:20.)

2. If only I had not urged the men to kill him.

Instead of a cycle of regret, Paul filled his mind with God's truth. He then made his past failures into a powerful life message.

BASIC GUIDELINES IN WRITING A LIFE MESSAGE

1. Have the right motive

The motive of your life message must be to glorify God, not yourself or your experiences, and certainly not your past failures.

2. Maintain a Life Notebook

There is great value in writing out your experiences. It will help you to look back on them at a later date and evaluate the lessons that God had in them. If they are written out, you will not lose or misrepresent important facts. Your life notebook will also be a valuable heritage for your children.

3. Have friends evaluate your testimony

Very often a person will give to a friend a detailed account of God's working in his life. Certain important points will stand out to his friend and cause him to rejoice in the report. All too often, however, when the friend urges him to repeat the testimony to another friend, significant points will be left out or reworded, and the effect of the testimony is greatly diminished.

4. Be careful to avoid certain dangers

- Do not describe details of immorality.
- Do not use words which stir up lustful thoughts.
- Do not repeat vulgar expressions.
- Do not refer to other people without their approval.
- Do not put others in a bad light.
- Do not make a joke of sin.
- Do not imitate mental or emotional or physical handicaps.
- Do not speak or write too soon after a failure.

5. Create interest in each point

Use curiosity to create interest in which you want to say. This is done by a question or a statement which will cause your listener to want to hear more. Rather than saying, "I envied my brother" say, "I secretly began doing something which damaged our relationship." Then go on to tell what you did.

6. Build your testimony around the principles of Scripture

Emphasize cause and effect sequences, and show how God's principles reveal the true working of human nature. For example, "When I began envying my brother, I got out from under the protection of my father's authority. I can now appreciate what happened in the emotions of Joseph's brothers. They resented him when he dreamed that one day they would bow down to him. Actually they were already emotionally bowing down to him, because of the fact that the one whom we envy controls us. When I envied my brother, he controlled my thought life, my digestive system, and my attitudes . . . ."

7. Evaluate the importance of your message

Ask yourself, "If I were listening, would I want to hear the rest of this message?" The listener will say yes if you relate your life message in terms of what he or she needs to hear. This should not be too difficult, since the temptations and struggles that you face are common to all. (See I Corinthians 10:13.) The length of your testimony should be carefully related to the schedule and interests of your listeners.

8. Be prepared for testing

Whenever you give a public testimony, you can expect to be tested on it. God's purpose through this testing is not to negate your testimony but to force you to see deeper and richer truths related to it.

WHAT IF I AM ALREADY DIVORCED AND REMARRIED?

Answer:

First, do not justify your divorce and remarriage. Acknowledge all guilt and ask for forgiveness from all who were offended.

Second, do not hide your divorce and remarriage. The fear that others will find out about it will hinder your friendships and your achievements.

Third, begin your own personal ministry of "rebuilding." Dedicate yourself to praying for couples who you know are considering divorce. Ask God for wisdom in giving appropriate exhortation to them. The success you have in saving or restoring marriages will gain for you proper acceptance by both pastors and laymen.

Years ago a father and mother divorced each other. The father married another woman. The new couple became active in church and saw all their children grow up and become active in Christian service. They also experienced obvious prosperity in their business.

One day their pastor reluctantly reported to them how their marriage was influencing other marriages in their church and in the community. "It is becoming increasingly difficult for me to talk couples in our church out of getting a divorce. They are all using you as their example."

The family met together to discuss the problem. Both the father and the stepmother had been counseled to marry each other; but each one acknowledged that, in order to do so, personal convictions had to be violated.

They decided to write a letter which the pastor could use when he counseled other couples. In this letter, they explained how they were wrong in the divorce and remarriage. They emphasized that any success which others might see in their marriage or family or business was not God's sanction on what they had done, but God's mercy on their repentant spirit.

They realized that this letter might open up questions by others and they began to formulate answers from the Scriptures. What they didn't expect was a new freedom from the pressures of the past and a joyful anticipation of the future. They also received greater grace from God because of their humility.

Additional benefits resulted in their own family. After the letter was written, one son exclaimed, "My whole attitude has changed toward my dad and my stepmother. I'm now proud of them for what they are doing."

10 HOW A LIFE MESSAGE CAN BE MORE FULFILLING THAN REMARRIAGE

Our fulfillment in life does not come by doing what we choose but by discovering and achieving the purposes for which God made us.

God made us primarily to have fellowship with Him and to be a witness of His truth. Since the testimony of Christ will be damaged by a remarriage, we can certainly expect God to give grace for the gift of singleness.

Fulfillment in life involves meeting basic needs. Some of these needs are:

The need for acceptance.
The need for future security.
The need to have meaningful fellowship with others.

Each of these needs, plus many more, can be fully met by allowing the Lord to develop an ever-growing, ever-deepening life message within us.

The more practical and helpful our life message, the more needed, secure, and appreciated we will be.

The security that results from an effective life message is valid for both single men and single women.

Often a divorced woman gets remarried for the purpose of future security, not realizing that her remarriage is actually destroying her future security. God has established that the ultimate security for a woman is not to be found in her family but in the local church which is fulfilling its Scriptural responsibility to Godly widows. If a woman remarries, however, she disqualifies herself from the church's responsibility. (See I Timothy 5:9.) No doubt one of the reasons for this requirement is to warn younger women to maintain God's marriage standards.

THE FULFILLING MESSAGE GOD DESIGNED FOR MATURE WOMEN

A woman whose husband has left her can continue to be very qualified to teach younger women.

God gives all Christian women the precise command to be ". . . teachers of good things" (Titus 2:3). He goes on to explain what these "good things" are. They make up a vital and valuable "seminar" for women:

TOPIC 1—Teach young women how to be serious-minded.
TOPIC 2—Teach young wives how to love their husbands.
TOPIC 3—Teach young mothers how to love their children.
TOPIC 4—Teach young women how to be discreet.
TOPIC 5—Teach young wives to be chaste.
TOPIC 6—Teach young mothers how to be "keepers at home."
TOPIC 7—Teach young women how to be Godly.
TOPIC 8—Teach young wives how to obey their husbands.

The importance of your teaching:

". . . *That the word of God be not blasphemed" (Titus 2:5).*

It is not difficult for a woman to love her husband when he loves her; but if she learns how to love her husband when he rejects her, then she has discovered Christ's genuine love. She has something valuable to teach younger women. The same is true for rearing children and for being discreet. When these responsibilities can be learned without the assistance of a husband, there will be valuable insights to add to the insights of other married women in effectively teaching younger women.

Rather than trying to find a new partner, a wise rebuilder should begin gathering material for an effective life message.

IMPORTANT GUIDELINES . . .

IN BECOMING A REBUILDER WITH THE GIFT OF SINGLENESS

A. See yourself as a "person," not as a "single." God made you in His own image. (See Genesis 1:27.)

B. Realize that you are "complete" in Christ, not an incomplete individual. (See Colossians 2:6-10.)

C. Develop your identity in terms of your relationship with Jesus Christ, not in terms of your associations with other people. (See I John 3:2.)

D. Enjoy your acceptance by God, rather than seeking the approval of others. (See Galatians 6:4.)

E. Remember that your purpose in life, whether single or married, is to glorify God, not to seek after your own happiness. (See I Corinthians 6:19-20.)

F. Recognize that your true happiness depends on your inward attitudes and character, not on outward circumstances or marital status. (See Matthew 5:3-12.)

G. Understand that your loneliness comes from desiring the fellowship of another more than the fellowship of God. (See Psalm 73:25.)

H. Look at your physical and family "defects" as God's special "marks of ownership" and "character-building motivations." (See II Corinthians 12:7-10.)

I. Realize that your power to live a victorious Christian life is related to your humility, and that physical "thorns in the flesh" are designed by God to produce the humility which results in the power of Christ. (See James 4:6-11.)

J. Learn to enjoy being alone by working on projects which you know will advance the work of God and benefit the lives of others. Be rich in good works! (See Titus 2:12-14.)

K. The unmarried man is free to care "... for the things that belong to the Lord, how he may please the Lord," whereas the married man must "... care for the things that are of the world, how he may please his wife" (I Corinthians 7:32-33).

L. Realize that the unmarried woman is free to care "... for the things of the Lord, that she may be holy both in body and in spirit: but she that is married careth for the things of the world, how she may please her husband" (I Corinthians 7:34).

M. Remember that God gives a special honor to those who put off marriage for the sake of more effective Christian service:

"... Neither let the eunuch say, Behold, I am a dry tree. For thus saith the Lord unto the eunuchs that keep my sabbaths, and choose the things that please me ... Even unto them will I give in mine house and within my walls a place and a name better than of sons and of daughters ..." (Isaiah 56:3-5).

N. Realize that the intensity of God-given marriage desires can be inflated and distorted by our own thoughts and actions. (See Proverbs 4:23.)

• Allowing our minds to dwell on marriage will increase our desires beyond their God-given levels. (See Hebrews 13:4.)

•Becoming involved in immoral actions will distort and ultimately pervert God-given marriage desires (See Ephesians 4:17-19.)

O. Use every thought that comes to your mind about marriage as a springboard to meditate on Scripture and God's character. (See II Corinthians 10:4-5.)

• God made you. Thank Him for the desires He gave you in His wisdom.

• God loves you. No good thing will He withhold from those who love Him.

• God knows you. He understands what will make you truly happy.

• God protects you. He wants to guard you from your own wrong desires.

• God provides for you. He fulfills needs you did not know you had.

P. Balance marriage expectations by listing the advantages of not being married. (See I Corinthians 7:32-35.)

• You are in the best position to discover how to be content in Christ.

• You are free from the continuing responsibilities of marriage.

- You can concentrate without distraction on the Lord's service.
- You have special motivations to learn patience, meekness, and self-control.

Answers to Quiz 6

(1) Abraham   (2) Adam   (3) David   (4) Paul

(5) Sarah   (6) Isaac   (7) Rachel   (8) Eve

A THRILLING, POWERFUL EXAMPLE
OF AN EFFECTIVE "LIFE MESSAGE"

"In 1976 I accepted Christ as my personal Savior and Lord in the midst of a family financial crisis and marital breakdown. Throughout, I and our three teen-aged children had prayed, worked, and hoped for reconciliation and reunion. But it was not to be—we were divorced in 1978 and my wife remarried.

"My children and I were devastated and heartbroken over these turns of events. My high hopes of being the husband of one wife and raising our children in the nurture and admonition of the Lord seemed to be utterly destroyed. At 39, my life was a complete shambles. Not only was I divorced, but I was homeless, jobless and deeply in debt. From a worldly perspective, my life appeared to be a complete wipe out—I was a man to be forgotten, quickly.

"But inwardly, God blessed me with the greatest personal victory one could ever hope for. The comfort and strength of the Holy Spirit will always be treasured; He gave me the power to forgive, a clear conscience, peace of heart and peace of mind concerning my hope of reconciliation, the continued love and respect of my children, and good health. Pearls at a great price, but pearls nonetheless.

"As much as this personal victory meant to me, I was still in shock and faced the frightening prospect of having to accept the fact that I was a divorced man living alone. Where does one begin? What do I do, especially when I can't even cook? And how do I deal with other women? They were beautiful and seemed to be everywhere all the time. God provided the direction before I had finished wondering about all this.

"An elder of my church met with me and pointed out in the Scriptures that God's best for me would be to remain single. That hit me like a punch in the nose! How could this be? I was the 'innocent party!' I had not wanted the divorce, had not encouraged it, and had indeed done all that I thought I could to prevent it. Now I was being told not to consider remarrying. It was a blow upon blows and just too big of a pill to swallow! However, within a few days another 'divine messenger' appeared. Some close friends gave me the 'Rebuilders' booklet published by the Institute in Basic Youth Conflicts which reinforced the same direction for my life. After reading it several times, I realized God was saying to me, 'This is the way, walk ye in it.' I promised God I would ponder it, but that was all. I wasn't ready to embrace that kind of a mind set. The press of the world was upon me then—I needed a job and a place to live, the bills needed to be paid, and I had a large monthly child support obligation to meet. I would come back to the rebuilder notion some other time.

"Within a matter of days after this, God provided an exciting new job in which He has helped 'rebuild' a shattered secular career. I soon found a place to live, which God furnished, and I got to the task of getting my budget under control and life in order. But then the notion of rebuilding was thrust upon me again when I ventured out into the 'singles' world. Much to my dismay, I was overwhelmed by the tragedy of it all. Again I found myself asking, how can this be? Why all this misery? The Church ought to do something about this!

"In the days that followed I began to note the significance of my circumstances. A very tight budget for the necessities of life prevented any kind of sustained, sophisticated dating life, let alone sufficient support to maintain two families if I remarried. But it did allow time to be alone with God and let the Holy Spirit, through the Word and Scriptural music, heal my broken heart. I also found my relationship with my children growing. It seemed that the turmoil and suffering we experienced had served only to deepen and strengthen our relationship. Additionally, while my former wife's family were not Christians, we were at peace. The original family spirit still existed and there was a great deal of freedom and flexibility to come and go when my children were with me. This was

(and is) important to everyone in the family. I realized another mate for me would break that unity of spirit and complicate life for all of us. I would have two mothers-in-law. I loved mine, but one was enough! The force of God's Word, the burden for the broken-hearted, plus the convenience of my circumstances were fast causing me to become a rebuilder at heart. What was I to do now?

"God soon lead me to appeal to my pastor to initiate a Rebuilder Program in our church. By now I was more than amazed at what I was doing and determined that if this was of God, then both my pastor and the board of elders would need to accept and bless this plan. If it were not of God, then that too would be made clear. They did so—enthusiastically! They were well aware of the great need—the focus on preventing divorce, reuniting broken marriages, and providing protection and direction to the divorced was eagerly received. God then quickly arranged for others with similar convictions (both married and divorced) to join me in further planning and prayer for someone to lead us. God answered our petitions with a full-time counselor-teacher and his wife. Our Rebuilder's Program was under way! What a victory!

"What a victory, indeed! Nothing in my life has been so thrilling, joyful and rewarding than to have participated in this undertaking and to have watched God put it all together. God's blessings have simply overtaken me. His intervention in my life to rebuild rather than remarry was an immense act of genuine love. He has healed my broken heart, and to the extent we can, my former wife and I have reconciled. All three of our children have accepted Christ as their personal Savior, and God has turned the heart of their stepfather to them. He also has provided funds to repay all my debts so that I am able to say I 'owe no man anything but to love one another.' As a result of all this He has given me the freedom, flexibility, and time to focus 'on the things of the Lord'— His Word and His people (my favorites are the fatherless). The 'leprosy' syndrome that a divorced person often carries with him vanished overnight when I appealed to my pastor. I saw that my church needed me! My place and ministry in the Body of Christ is in the middle of a program that strengthens existing marriages and rebuilds broken ones. (That is exactly what is happening! Under the hand of our counselor-teacher and his wife, three divorced couples are being reunited in marriage.) As a rebuilder I find myself encompassed in a circle of love that yields comfort, companionship, encouragement, and a renewed purpose for living. There is such a sense of peace and contentment about it all that I would not trade places with anyone, anywhere, anytime. And my 'Plan A,' which I thought was utterly destroyed, remains in effect. I'm still the husband of one wife and will continue to raise (teach) my children in the ways of the Lord. The urgency and need to do the latter is even greater now than before, and it is being done by the grace of the Lord Jesus Christ. His grace is sufficient for me. Indeed, it is such that I now rejoice in my weaknesses and infirmities (in being a divorced man, living alone) that the Spirit and power of Christ (in being a rebuilder) may rest upon me."

Used by permission

Personal Commitment and Accountability

In rebuilding past failures into a new life message:

- ☐ 1. I purpose to concentrate on building an effective life message so that I can help others with the life-changing principles that God is teaching me.

- ☐ 2. I am committed to making sure that my life message is carefully prepared so that it will fully glorify God.

- ☐ 3. If I am remarried, I have purposed to respect the continuing limitations in Christian leadership of not being a "bishop or deacon."

- ☐ 4. If I am not remarried, I have purposed to accept the limitation of singleness as God's gift and guidance for more effective and fruitful Christian service.

- ☐ 5. I have purposed to have the following person evalute my life message:

- ☐ 6. I have purposed to check out my life message with each person mentioned in it.

- ☐ 7. I have purposed to strengthen my heart by reading the biographies of the men and women in God's "Hall of Fame."

Signed _____ Date _____

MY NEW LIFE MESSAGE

MY NEW LIFE MESSAGE

GOAL NUMBER **7**

REBUILDING THE DAMAGED MARRIAGES OF OTHERS

"Brethren, if any of you do err from the truth, and one convert him; Let him know, that he which converteth the sinner from the error of his way, shall save a soul from death, and shall hide a multitude of sins."

James 5:19-20

REBUILDER'S QUIZ

Do you know how to respond to the dangers of giving counsel?

Dangers:

1. Interfering with the God-ordained authorities of the one you counsel.
2. Having the one whom you counsel fall in love with you.
3. Falling in love with the one whom you try to counsel.
4. Wasting many hours talking to those who are not serious.
5. Causing a satanic reaction against you or your family.
6. Being used by those you try to counsel to agree with their wrong ideas.
7. Getting into discussions about your personal opinions.
8. Becoming embroiled in fruitless arguments.

9. Allowing those you counsel to become too dependent on you.

Match the right response to the corresponding danger:

a. Re-affirm the decision that you will not date.
b. Bind Satan in prayer before you try to free one under his power.
c. Do not respond to hypothetical situations.
d. Avoid foolish and unlearned questions.
e. Teach those you help how to get answers from the Bible.
f. Use only God's Word when you counsel.
g. Limit the time you talk and require that an assigned project be finished before the next talk.
h. Find out who is spiritually responsible for the one who asks for counsel and work through them.
i. Never counsel a person of the opposite sex. Work through the partner or parents.

See answers on page 247.

God has established the local church to be His standard-bearer for truth. When the Church moves forward in the truth and power of the Holy Spirit against the forces of darkness, even "... the gates of hell shall not prevail against it" (Matthew 16:18).

A rebuilder must be committed to getting under the spiritual authority of a Bible-believing local church, and doing everything possible to strengthen its ministry and outreach.

The foundations of a strong and effective local church are the marriages and families within the church. "If the foundations be destroyed, what can the righteous do" (Psalm 11:3).

1. See the vision of your ministry

One of the most important and urgently needed church ministries of our day is the ministry of rebuilding marriages. For most rebuilders, it will begin as a part-time ministry. Then, for many, it will flourish into a full-time ministry among families in the church and in the community.

A rebuilder's ministry includes . . .

1. Being a consistent, living example of a happy, fulfilled, victorious, and fruitful Christian.

   "... *Be thou an example of the believers, in word, in conversation, in charity, in spirit, in faith, in purity*" (I Timothy 4:12).

2. Having a working knowledge of the principles and testimonies of the Bible that are related to marriage, divorce, and remarriage.

   "*Study to shew thyself approved unto God, a workman that needeth not to be ashamed, rightly dividing the word of truth*" (II Timothy 2:15).

3. Giving clear, loving, and patient testimony for God's true and just standards of marriage.

   "And the servant of the Lord must not strive; but be gentle unto all men, apt to teach, patient" (II Timothy 2:24).

4. Explaining to those who are considering divorce and remarriage the deception and destruction of today's "fairness theology."

   "In meekness instructing those that oppose themselves; if God peradventure will give them repentance to the acknowledging of the truth" (II Timothy 2:25).

5. Encouraging your church to establish Scriptural policies which will discourage divorce and remarriage.

   ". . . What therefore God hath joined together, let not man put asunder" (Matthew 19:6).

6. Watching for failing marriages and working out creative ways of strengthening them and their families.

   "And let us consider one another to provoke unto love and to good works" (Hebrews 10:24).

7. Teaching those who are already divorced or remarried how they can become effective rebuilders.

   ". . . He hath sent me to bind up the brokenhearted, to proclaim liberty to the captives, and the opening of the prison to them that are bound" (Isaiah 61:1).

2. Work through each Rebuilder's Goal

Concentrate on the first six goals in this manual. Implement these goals as fully as you can in your life, realizing that they will be continuing and growing projects for years to come.

The key word for success is "accountability." Work with one who can check up on your progress and consistency. God commands us to ". . . exhort one another daily, while it is called To-day; lest any of you be hardened through the deceitfulness of sin" (Hebrews 3:13).

The more you work through the first six goals, the more effective your rebuilder's testimony will become.

3. Meet with your pastor

- Set up a meeting with your pastor or one of the elders of the church.
- Tell him that you have committed yourself to being a rebuilder. Explain what a rebuilder is.
- Share your testimony with your pastor and also give him a written copy of it.
- Explain that you are willing to assist in any way you can to encourage other divorced people to become rebuilders.
- Suggest the idea of a "Rebuilder's Class" in the church. Explain the potential of reaching out in the community to those who are divorced. Show how the *Rebuilder's Guide* could be used as the outline for sessions.
- Inquire about the possibility of the official church board approving a rebuilder's group as a part of the ministry of the church.
- Offer to share your testimony before the church. Ask that the church have a special prayer of dedication for your ministry of rebuilding.

<table>
<tr><td>

2

</td><td>

PRAY THAT THE CHURCH WILL ADOPT SOUND MARRIAGE POLICIES

</td></tr>
</table>

Countless marriages could be saved if each local church had clear policies that would prohibit unscriptural marriages from being performed in the church.

Here are three recommended policies which would accomplish this:

1. BOTH PARTIES MUST BE CHRISTIANS

In view of God's clear command not to be "unequally yoked together with unbelievers," we will not marry a believer with a non-believer. (See II Corinthians 6:14-18; Amos 3:3; I Corinthians 7:39.)

2. BOTH MUST HAVE PARENTS' CONSENT

In view of God's command to honor and obey parents and not to forsake their counsel, we will not marry a couple unless the parents on both sides are in full harmony with the marriage. (See Exodus 20:12; Proverbs 30:17; Proverbs 6:20; Proverbs 23:22.)

3. NEITHER ONE CAN BE DIVORCED

In view of the spiritual meaning and message of marriage which the church is committed to preserving, and in view of the vows which a married person has made, we will not marry a divorced person whose former partner is still living. (See I Corinthians 7:11, 16, 39; Romans 7:1-3; Ephesians 5:21-33; Luke 16:17-18.)

WHAT HAPPENS WHEN DIVORCED PEOPLE ARE REMARRIED IN THE CHURCH

CONSEQUENCES TO THE REMARRIED PERSONS

1. Pressure to justify their remarriage

People who have divorced and remarried tend to feel the need to explain why they remarried. Their attempts to justify their remarriage puts them on the defensive and causes them to blame their former partners. They also tend to work for acceptance by involving themselves in extra activity in the church.

2. Conflict in other relationships

If people reject the "character school" of their first marriage, God will be forced to raise up another "classroom." The second classroom will involve different people and greater conflicts.

3. Physical weakness, sickness, and death

A lack of thorough self-examination will result in the Lord's chastening. "For this cause many are weak and sickly among you, and many sleep [have died]" (I Corinthians 11:30). (See also James 5:14-16.)

CONSEQUENCES TO THE CHURCH

1. Damage to the picture of basic truths

Since marriage is an object lesson of important spiritual truths, these truths are damaged when marriages are broken and remarriages are performed in the church. (See Goal Number Two.)

2. Encouragement for more divorces

When divorced people tell how happy and blessed of God they have been since getting remarried, many others who have unhappy marriages will be prompted to follow their example.

3. Distortion of truth by remarried people who teach in the church

- Some remarried teachers will take a weak position regarding divorce and remarriage in order not to condemn themselves.

- Other remarried teachers will be too harsh and unloving toward those who have been divorced and remarried. They will condemn themselves also.

- Some remarried teachers will seek to justify their remarriage by distorting or misinterpreting what the Bible actually teaches about divorce and remarriage.

- Other remarried teachers will tell shameful details about their first marriage in order to win sympathy and acceptance for their divorce and remarriage.

These distortions can be eliminated if the person who has divorced and remarried becomes an effective rebuilder before being given an opportunity to teach in the church.

THE UNEXPECTED CONSEQUENCES IN THE COMMUNITY WHEN REMARRIAGES OCCUR IN THE CHURCH

"I have been a pastor for over thirty years. My present church has a membership of two thousand people.

"When I entered the ministry, it was rare for me to receive a request to marry a divorced person. I turned down these requests on the basis of the marriage vows and the many Scripture passages which forbid such remarriages.

"As the number of divorces increased in our nation, however, more and more pressure was put upon me to conduct marriage ceremonies for divorced people. Special pressure came from new Christians who were divorced before they were converted and also from the sons and daughters of some of the leading church families.

The death of a conviction

"Finally, I consented to marry one divorced person. This person convinced me that his divorce was on 'Scriptural grounds,' and therefore it was also Scripturally right to remarry someone else.

"This marriage opened the door for other marriages of divorced people. Soon the Scriptural teachings on marriage, divorce, and remarriage were blurred in my mind.

"When a divorced person asked me to perform a wedding ceremony, I would ask some questions and listen intently for 'Biblical reasons' for the divorce. However, even after hearing them, my heart was always heavy after these weddings. I would wonder what my Heavenly Father thought about these ceremonies.

"In spite of this, I still defended my position on divorce and remarriage. When I attended my first Basic Youth Seminar in 1972, I learned a great deal; but when Bill indicated his position against divorce and remarriage, I found my mind arguing with him. After the sessions, I encountered some of his staff members and presented my arguments to them.

The seeds of disintegration

"Soon I began to notice several trends in my church. I noticed that the majority of those who remarried had a very difficult time making their second marriage work. I was forced to spend many hours with them in counseling. The more I counseled, the more I saw the complications of a second marriage.

"One of the major conflicts of a second marriage involved the children. A constant flow of conflicts resulted from their difficulty in accepting their new parent.

"However, the most disturbing trend I observed was a great increase in divorces among the couples of my own church. Many of these couples had been unhappy in their marriages, and they thought that others who had divorced and remarried were now happy. They didn't know what I knew about these second marriages.

The witness of two rebuilders

"One day last year, I was invited by a divorced couple to meet with them and eight other pastors and their wives. We all listened in amazement as this couple opened up their hearts to us.

"We all knew this couple and respected them. They appeared to have a very happy and successful second marriage. Now they were explaining to us how they knew that their second marriage was against God's teachings even though God had richly blessed them and their family.

"This couple wanted us to know that God's blessing on their lives was not a vindication of what they had done, but rather God's mercy upon them for their repentant spirit.

"They explained how sad they were to know that their success and happiness were causing others with unhappy marriages to consider divorce and remarriage. They no longer wanted to influence others to break their marriage vows. They pleaded with us to take a strong stand against divorce and remarrage. Then they gave us copies of their testimony which we could use with other couples.

"This was a painful meeting for them, but what a witness to us pastors! I went home and re-read all the material on the subject of marriage which had been sent to me by the Institute in Basic Youth Conflicts.

"One new fact was now very clear to me. I could not shake it from my mind. Every time I performed a ceremony for divorced people, everyone in my church and community could say, 'See, the pastor is marrying divorced people, so he must approve of divorce and remarriage. When I get fed up with my marriage, I'll find a new partner and get the approval of the pastor and the church. If I get their approval, I will surely have God's approval, too!'

"Soon, a second disturbing thought was added to the first one. I remembered my frequent exhortations to the many young people of our church, 'Marriage is for keeps! Take the word "divorce" out of your vocabulary. God can solve any marriage problem!' I began to wonder what they thought when they saw me marrying divorced people!

"After further study and prayer, I purposed to return to my original conviction of not marrying divorced people. This was a difficult decision because I have a very large number of divorced people in my church, and many of them are single and hoping to remarry.

"I came before the deacons and explained that I now had clear personal convictions against marrying any divorced person and asked them if they would stand with me on these convictions.

"The chairman of the board expressed his wholehearted support and offered to answer the questions of anyone in the church who had questions about the pastor's stand. All the other deacons also supported my stand.

"Any conviction will be tested, and this conviction was no exception. A few people began to put a great deal of pressure on me. The Lord had his own way of reinforcing the stand that I had taken.

The confirming event

"A young Christian in the church noticed a pick-up truck with some large tires in the back of it. He was looking for tires like that, so he decided to stop and ask the truck owner about them.

"The pick-up truck was parked in front of a small store. He went inside and saw only one man. That man was standing by a magazine rack looking at a pornographic magazine.

"The young Christian walked up to the man and asked him if he owned the pick-up truck outside. The man closed the magazine and responded to the questions.

"As the conversation continued, the truck owner finally said, 'Say, there are some pretty hot things in this magazine. You ought to get one.'

"The young Christian explained that since he became a Christian and joined my church, he didn't read magazines like that anymore. An angry look came over the truck owner's face as he blurted out, 'I used to go to your church all the time until I got real bitter toward your church and your pastor!'

"The Christian was shocked and asked him, 'Why did you get bitter?'

"He replied, 'Well, my wife and I had just gotten a divorce. I loved her and was really hoping that we could put our marriage back together someday. She started to date someone in your church. Your pastor never tried to rebuild our marriage. He just married her to this new guy! It really made me bitter!'

"The young Christian explained that the pastor does not marry divorced people anymore and invited the man to attend church with him. The truck owner said that since the pastor had changed his position on marrying divorced people, he would consider coming to the church."

Used by permission

BASIC GUIDELINES

IN TALKING TO A FRIEND WHO WANTS TO DIVORCE OR REMARRY

1. Before you begin couseling, determine your goals

- To prevent God's name from being blasphemed among unbelievers. (See Titus 2:5; I Timothy 6:1; Romans 2:24.)
- To identify the real causes of the conflicts. (See Hebrews 12:15-17.)
- To view the conflict as character-building lessons. (See Romans 8:28-29.)

2. Work with those responsible for your friend

Your first step is to find out who is spiritually responsible for your friend, and then to work with them. With your friend's permission, contact the husband, parents, or parents-in-law. Ask if they would like you to assist them in this matter. Parents are still responsible for their sons and daughters after marriage, because God commands them to teach their children and their children's children. (See Deuteronomy 4:9.)

3. Bind Satan before you "spoil his house"

If your friend is bound by wrong attitudes or wrong reasonings, you are not just dealing with "flesh and blood" but with spiritual powers. (See Ephesians 6:12.) In order to conquer, you must bind Satan's power over your friend and then cast down false reasoning and bring every thought into captivity to the obedience of Christ. (See II Corinthians 10:4-5.)

4. Get the facts before giving any counsel

God warns that it is folly to try to answer a problem before you learn all the basic facts related to it. (See Proverbs 18:13.) Use the questions on the following pages to gain the necessary background information. As you ask the questions, discern the attitudes of your friend and the root causes of the conflicts.

5. Never listen to sensual details

You will damage your own thought life if you allow your friend to tell you any details of immoral actions. Your imagination will fill in the details and make your friend's sin attractive to you. For this and other reasons, "... it is a shame even to speak of those things which are done of them in secret (Ephesians 5:12).

6. Avoid listening to bad reports

Obviously, your friend will expect you to agree with his or her decision to obtain a divorce. Thus your friend will often try to give you as much information as possible against the partner. You will be expected to agree that a divorce is the only answer. However, your purpose is not to build a case against the other partner, but to help your friend see his or her own faults and to understand God's higher purposes in allowing the conflicts to occur. (See I Peter 3:14-18.)

7. Establish "God's best" as your friend's goal

Early in the conversation, ask your friend if he or she really wants God's best for the marriage and family. This is important because it gives you the basis for explaining the disciplines which God requires in order to achieve His best: dying to self, suffering for righteousness' sake, yielding rights, fully forgiving, gaining a clear conscience, and winning by love.

8. Look at conflicts as character training

Marriage is God's "classroom," and your friend's marriage conflicts are simply the "lessons" that God is giving in order to teach more about Him so that your friend will become more conformed to the image of His Son, Jesus Christ. It is only on this basis that God promises that "... all things work together for good to them that love God, to them who are the called according to his purpose. For whom he did foreknow, he also did predestinate to be conformed to the image of his Son, that he might be the firstborn among many brethren" (Romans 8:28-29).

Your job is to help your friend discover how marriage disappointments and pressures can be used to build Godly character. The reward is not only the wisdom and glory of God, but the removal of the pressures, because God makes our enemies to be at peace with us when our ways please Him. (See Proverbs 16:7.)

9. See your friend as the key to the solution

It is easy to assume that your friend's partner or parents or parents-in-law must change before your friend can have a happy marriage. This is not true. Your friend has the potential through God of changing the entire situation.

If your friend is the husband, you must help him realize that he is the "strong man" of his house and that he can ask God to build a "hedge of protection" around his family and reclaim that which has been taken captive by Satan. (See Mark 3:27; Job 1:10.)

If your friend is the wife, you must help her realize that she has the spiritual power to win her husband by Godly character—even though the husband rejects God's Word. (See I Peter 3:1-6.)

10. Appeal to the conscience of your friend

To appeal to one's conscience is to point out the personal responsibilities an individual has in a given situation. For example, the partner may have been unloving, but your friend is responsible under God to return love for hate and good for evil.

When you point out from Scripture that your friend is responsible for his or her own thoughts (II Corinthians 10:5), words (Matthew 12:36), actions (Romans 2:1-11), and motives (Jeremiah 17:10), you prompt Godly conviction. This, in turn, will lead to repentance and humility. God can then give a fresh measure of His grace to resolve marriage conflicts in His way.

LEARN HOW TO ASK PRECISE QUESTIONS

QUESTIONS	BASIS FOR QUESTIONS
1. Do you want God's best for your life, marriage, and family?	Those seeking help must begin by wanting to achieve God's highest purposes for them whatever the cost. Every Christian can achieve God's highest goals by entering into Christ's power and becoming like Him. To experience God's perfect will in our lives, we must usually do just the opposite of our natural inclinations. "There is a way which seemeth right unto a man, but the end thereof are the ways of death" (Proverbs 14:12).
2. Are you already physically or emotionally involved with someone else?	All too often this is the case. The person is looking for reasons to get out of the marriage, not to stay in it. This person must be confronted with the fact that he or she is already guilty of the adultery. "...Whosoever looketh on a woman to lust after her hath committed adultery with her already in his heart" (Matthew 5:28).
3. When you were married, did you vow "...for better, for worse, 'til death do us part?"	A person is only as good as his or her word: "For by thy words thou shalt be justified, and by thy words thou shalt be condemned" (Matthew 12:37). God will require of us every vow we make. (See Ecclesiastes 5:4-6.)
4. Do you know why God hates divorce?	Divorce destroys the symbolic picture of Christ's relationship with the Church, which every marriage is to represent. (See Ephesians 5:21-33.) Divorce destroys the foundation of society and allows blasphemy against the Word of God. (See Titus 2:5.) Divorce damages the lives of children for generations to come. (See Malachi 2:13-16.)

5. When did you become a Christian?

6. Since becoming a Christian, have you discovered how to enter into Christ's power for Christian living?

7. Have you ever fully dedicated your body as a living sacrifice to God?

8. Did you marry with the full consent of your parents and your parents-in-law?

9. What are the main reasons that you want a divorce? (List the reasons.)

Never take your salvation for granted. Often God's purpose in marital conflicts is to use these conflicts to bring one or both parties to repentance and true salvation.

A person who claims to be a Christian but continues to live in lust or hatred must search his heart to find out whether he really is a Christian. "Whosoever hateth his brother is a murderer: and ye know that no murderer hath eternal life abiding in him" (I John 3:15).

Many Christians are totally defeated and discouraged because they are trying to live the Christian life in the power of their own minds, wills, and emotions (soul power), rather than in the power of Christ's victory over the world, the flesh, and the devil. (See Romans 6:1-15.) (See Goal Number One.)

Once a Christian grasps the fact that he or she died with Christ and rose again with Him, Romans 12:1-2 can become a reality in his or her life: ". . . Present your bodies a living sacrifice, holy, acceptable unto God . . . ." Then every day the members of our body must be yielded to God as instruments of righteousness. (See Romans 6:13.)

God warns that if the counsel of parents is not honored, things will not go well for us. "Honour thy father and mother . . . That it may be well with thee . . ." (Ephesians 6:2-3). If the wishes of your parents were violated, you must ask your parents for their forgiveness.

If the person is sincere, these reasons will give you a basis for providing Scriptural insight and direction. The reasons will usually reveal wrong attitudes, unwillingness to suffer for righteousness' sake, lack of faith in God's power, lack of understanding of God's purposes through tribulation, or lack of power to live the Christian life.

QUESTIONS	BASIS FOR QUESTIONS
10. In addition to these reasons, are there any others?	Before responding to any of the reasons in Question 9, ask Question 10. Usually people will give you the "surface" reason first and hesitate to tell you the "root" reason. The root reason may be some secret sin, fear, or goal. Without knowing it and dealing with it, you will waste a great deal of time and not get lasting results.
11. What do you think that God is trying to say to you through your marriage conflicts?	The best way to solve a conflict is to see it in its bigger perspective. Is God using conflicts to motivate the person to confess secret sin? "He that covereth his sins shall not prosper: but whoso confesseth and forsaketh them shall have mercy" (Proverbs 28:13). Is God using the conflict to develop the character of Christ in them? "... Tribulation worketh patience; And patience, experience; and experience, hope: And hope maketh not ashamed; because the love of God is shed abroad in our hearts by the Holy Ghost which is given unto us" (Romans 5:3-5).
12. If I were to ask your partner to list your faults, what would be listed?	It is very important to learn to see conflicts through the eyes of both partners. Only as this is done will the proper basis be laid for repentance, humility, grace, and lasting solutions. "Every way of a man is right in his own eyes: but the Lord pondereth the hearts" (Proverbs 21:2). "He that is first in his own cause seemeth just; but his neighbour cometh and searcheth him" (Proverbs 18:17).
13. Are you aware of the destructive consequences of getting a divorce?	The following material should be shared with anyone who is contemplating a divorce *after* the previous questions have been asked and responded to.

6 | WHEN A WIFE INITIATES A DIVORCE

WHAT ARE THE CONSEQUENCES?

1. She exposes herself to Satan's power

God emphasizes that when a person willfully gets out from under the human authority He has provided, that person is committing a sin whose consequences are the same as those of witchcraft. (See I Samuel 15:23.)

Witchcraft exposes a person to the reality and power of Satan's control. It is for this very reason that God warns every person to be under His authority. (See Romans 13:1-6.)

Wives are instructed to submit to their own husbands. (See Ephesians 5:22, I Peter 3:1.) This means that they are to "get under the protection of their own husbands."

The alternative to Scriptural submission is not freedom, but defeat by Satan and exploitation by others.

2. She destroys many families

By disobeying God's Word and taking matters into her own hands, the wife destroys both her own family and her husband's family. She sows the seeds of destruction in the families of her children and her grandchildren "to the third and fourth generation." (See Deuteronomy 5:9.)

She also sows the seeds of destruction in the families of those who were looking to her as an example of loyalty and endurance. If her husband remarries, there are usually additional destructive results.

3. She causes others to sin by taking sides

When a wife initiates a divorce, she forces her children to take sides. As they take up offenses for her or against her, they violate Scripture and establish the roots of deep bitterness (Psalm 15:3).

Also, by getting out from under her husband's authority, she puts herself on an equal level with her husband. This causes further divisions between her children since they now have "two masters," and "no man can serve two masters: for either he will hate the one, and love the other; or else he will hold to the one, and despise the other..." (Matthew 6:24).

4. She proves that she has a hard heart

When the Pharisees tried to justify divorce, they asked why Moses provided for divorce in the Old Testament Law. Jesus answered, "... Moses because of the hardness of your hearts suffered you to put away your wives: but from the beginning it was not so" (Matthew 19:8).

5. She blasphemes the Word of God

God is very concerned that His Name not be blasphemed among unbelievers. (See II Samuel 12:14; I Timothy 6:1.) God commands wives to love their husbands and to be obedient to them "... that the Word of God be not blasphemed" (Titus 2:5).

By divorcing her husband, a wife is doing just the opposite of loving her husband and being obedient to him.

6. She exposes her family to greater temptations

By divorcing her husband, a wife exposes him to a greater temptation of immorality with other women; and by getting out from under her husband's protection, she also exposes her children to unnecessary temptation. (See I Corinthians 7:14.)

7. She balances guilt with blame

In order to justify her action of divorcing her husband, a wife must constantly remind herself of his offenses. This only deepens her bitterness and reinforces her guilt.

She also causes guilt and bitterness in her children and in any others who take up offenses for or against her.

8. She destroys a vital witness of truth

Marriage is a "human object lesson" of God's relationship with Israel and Christ's relationship with the Church. (See Ephesians 5:21-33.) Anyone who destroys this object lesson is damaging not only God's established order for marriage and the family, but a vital witness of God's truth to the world.

9. She damages her children's heritage

When a mother suffers for doing right, she is providing by her example a Godly heritage for her children. She is teaching them how to respond to hurts and disappointments. She is also able to let them see Christ's character formed in her by rightly responding to suffering. (See I Peter 4:12-19.)

10. She rejects the power of God

God has assured us that He is greater than any force or influence we may have to cope with. (See I John 4:4.) He has promised not to allow us to be tempted above that which we are able to endure. (See I Corinthians 10:13.) He has taught us how to take hold of His spiritual weapons and be victorious. (See Ephesians 6:12-18.) Divorce is a public rejection of all these truths and provisions.

11. She confirms that she has a dominant will

In order for a woman to divorce her husband, she must first get out from under his authority and then take matters into her own hands. In so doing, she puts herself above her husband and becomes his judge. Such action exposes the fact that she has not only a willful spirit, but also pride, since only by pride cometh contention. . ." (Proverbs 13:10).

12. She allows God's enemies to justify their sin

When Christians fail to live up to God's moral standards, non-Christians are able to justify their own standards as being equal to or better than those of Christians. The hypocrisy of Christians is no excuse for sinners; nevertheless, it is being used by Satan to keep many from eternal life.

13. She takes vengeance into her own hands

Divorce is a form of vengeance against a marriage partner. When a wife uses it, she violates God's direct plea and command: "Dearly beloved, avenge not yourselves, but rather give place unto wrath: for it is written, Vengeance is mine; I will repay, saith the Lord" (Romans 12:19).

14. She is judged by others

When a wife judges her husband by divorcing him, God promises that she will be judged by others. "Judge not, that ye be not judged. For with what judgment ye judge, ye shall be judged: and with what measure ye mete, it shall be measured to you again" (Matthew 7:1-2).

15. She suffers leanness in her soul

A wife may try to justify herself in divorcing her husband, and God may allow her to obtain the desires of her heart as a result of the divorce, but He will also decrease her capacity to know and enjoy Him and His ways. She will become like those to whom ". . . he gave . . . their request; but sent leanness into their soul" (Psalm 106:15).

THE COUNSEL OF AN ATTORNEY

"You will recall that we discussed the situation of divorce and remarriage and I wanted to encourage you to maintain the strong stand and Scriptural position that you have taken. I have recently had a number of cases and probate proceedings where much bitterness existed between the families of remarried individuals. I personally had approximately four or five matters in Probate Court for families that had a strong Christian testimony. However, there was divorce and remarriage in one instance, and death and remarriage in the other backgrounds. In each instance, there were children born of both families or stepchildren. Following the death of the male married partner, there was much bitterness that developed between the surviving wife and the children of the deceased husband. The children did not believe that they obtained a fair share of the estate and looked upon the remarried spouse as an intruder into the estate or the family earned by their father and divorced or deceased mother. On several occasions, the divorced spouse took up the offense and attempted to become involved in the estate for the children.

"Without getting into the details of the specifics, there are many underlying problems, difficulties, offenses, and bitternesses yet to come into existence on the issue of divorce and remarriage. Right now, the sociologist and Christian community are seeing the direct effect and that is the immediate effect on finances, testimony, and children. However, the future result is yet to be seen and even when a remarriage appears to be working and blessed of God, there can be stepchildren and relatives with offenses existing because of the divorce or because of the remarriage that are simply waiting to exhibit their offenses after the death of one of the remarried parties when it then comes into fruition. Consequently, the shock waves of divorce and remarriage are obviously more troublesome for one generation, irrespective of the poor testimony, but the direct effect of the offense and judgment for hardness of heart runs headlong into the next generation old enough to take up the offense.

Used by permission

WHAT ARE THE CONSEQUENCES?

1. God will destroy the work of his hands

A man forfeits his potential for success when he divorces his wife. By violating his marriage vows, he invites the judgment of God upon the work of his hands. (See Ecclesiastes 5:6.)

2. He allows sinners to blaspheme God's name

When Christians fail to live by the high standards of Scripture, "... the name of God is blasphemed among the Gentiles ..." (Romans 2:24). Those who reject God's moral standards are able to justify themselves when they see a Christian violate God's marriage standards.

3. He causes others to judge him

Divorce is a judgment against one's partner. It is the opposite of discernment and restoration. For this reason God warns that anyone who judges another will be judged, because he is guilty of the very same things. (See Romans 2:1-3.)

4. He proves that he lacks genuine love

The Lord Jesus clearly explained to the wicked Pharisees that anyone who divorces his wife is guilty of "hardness of heart" (See Matthew 19:8.) Genuine love, however, "... suffereth long ... Beareth all things ... endureth all things" (I Corinthians 13:4-8).

5. He suffers leanness in his soul

A man who divorces his wife may get what he wants, but God will send leanness to his soul (See Psalm 106:15.) This will cause him to lack the desire and power to comprehend the "meat of the Word" or to be conformed to the image of Christ. (See Romans 8:29; Hebrews 5:12-14.)

6. He causes his wife to commit adultery

Christ very clearly teaches that a husband who divorces his wife is guilty of causing her to commit adultery if she becomes physically involved with another man. ". . . Whosoever shall put away his wife, saving for the cause of fornication, causeth her to commit adultery . . ." (Matthew 5:32).

7. He denies his children vital training

Children should be able to see how their father deals with marriage conflicts according to Scriptural principles, and how he uses them as a means of developing humility and Godly character. (See I Timothy 4:12.)

8. He forces his children to choose sides

By separating himself from his wife, a man forces his children to divide their loyalties. His action prompts them to take up offenses and become deeply bitter. When parents fight, children have "two masters," and "no man can serve two masters: for either he will hate the one, and love the other; or else he will hold to the one, and despise the other . . ." (Matthew 6:24).

9. He sows seeds of guilt and bitterness

His action not only brings deep guilt and bitterness upon himself, but also sows seeds of guilt and bitterness in his wife, children, parents, parents-in-law, and close friends on both sides of the marriage.

10. He fails to be a man of his word

A man is only as good as his word. That is why a man will be judged by his words. "For by thy words thou shalt be justified, and by thy words thou shalt be condemned" (Matthew 12:37).

11. He disqualifies himself from church leadership

A man proves that he is unfit for church leadership if he cannot manage his own family. "For if a man know not how to rule his own house, how shall he take care of the church of God" (I Timothy 3:5).

12. He destroys the message of marriage

The spiritual message of marriage is to demonstrate Christ's love for the Church. Christ is not going to divorce His Bride, the Church, even though she is adulterous. (See Ephesians 5:22-32.)

13. He fails to "cleanse his wife" by Scripture

God holds a husband responsible for purifying his wife's desires, attitudes, and actions by using the Scriptures. He is to "sanctify and cleanse" her by God's Word (Ephesians 5:25-26.)

14. He is guilty of taking God's vengeance

When a man divorces his wife, he is taking vengeance into his own hands and doing what only God can do. ". . . Vengeance is mine; I will repay, saith the Lord" (Romans 12:19).

15. He forfeits the purification of suffering

Conflicts in marriage cause suffering. However, God has designed this suffering to purify the husband's motives and character so that God can reward him with the glory of His own wisdom and grace (See I Peter 4:1, 12-13.)

16. He exposes himself to new temptations

God wants a man's sexual drives to be fulfilled within marriage. (I Corinthians 7:1-9.) When a husband divorces his wife, he becomes extremely vulnerable to temptations of impure thoughts and actions with other women.

17. He dishonors his parents

Divorce is a public shame to the parents. It damages their name and forces them to bear the sorrow and shame of failure with a son. God has severe warnings for dishonoring parents. (See Proverbs 20:20, Matthew 15:4.)

THE TESTIMONY OF AN ATTORNEY

"I am a practicing attorney and have been in general practice for ten years. The first five years of my practice were before I became a Christian. My practice was a general one and approximately thirty-five percent of our work was directly related to domestic and personal (divorce) matters.

"While attending Bible Study Fellowship in the Fall of 1976, I began to study the Bible and I found it to be a very perplexing book, especially since I did not know the Author. In February, 1977, my wife and I were invited by my brother, who is a physician, to attend a Christian Fellowship retreat. It was there that God's Holy Spirit convicted me of my sin and convinced me that I was not saved. That night I prayed to receive Jesus as my Lord and Savior. My wife had been saved two years prior to the retreat.

"From February 26, 1977, I began to engulf the Word of God. My brother and other Christian friends encouraged my wife and me to attend a Basic Seminar in March of 1977. We attended the entire week, and God used His Word to direct us in many aspects of our life. From that week forward, I began to question what God's will was for me in my law practice, specifically in the area of divorce. I struggled with the Lord for about two years. In July of 1979, God finally convinced me, after much deliberation, that He doesn't like divorce—in fact, He hates it (Malachi 2:16).

"It became so clear what God meant in Genesis when He said, 'Therefore shall a man leave his father and his mother, and shall cleave unto his wife: and they shall be one flesh' (Genesis 2:24).

"The first Seminar apprised me that it was better not to make a vow, than to make one and break it (Ecclesiates 5:4-5). Further, Matthew 19:6 clearly states, '. . . What therefore God hath joined together, let not man put asunder.' I truly did not desire to be 'that man.'

"God brought me into an intense study of His Word on the subject of divorce, and no matter what any man could say or what excuse human reasoning would entice, in my spirit, I knew what I was doing was wrong in God's sight and not in accordance with His Word. I now had a serious problem to face. My partner and I had made almost $70,000 in divorce cases alone in the first half of 1979. I was certainly hesitant to tell him of my decision to no longer handle divorces. After much prayer, we met and talked about my decision, at which time I advised him that I would not file another divorce for any person, Christian or non-

Christian. I further explained that God had greatly convicted me that our earthly marriage was to be for life and was to portray the greatest marriage that will ever take place—when Jesus, the Bridegroom, comes back to take His Church, the Bride, to be with Him forever.

"My partner was very understanding, but as any conscientious partner, he was apprehensive about the loss of my part of the revenue for the remainder of the year. I had to come to the place in my life where the loss of income was not my motivation, but to do the will of my Father was my utmost desire. When I gave my life to Jesus back in 1977, I gave my law practice and everything I owned to God. He became my Supplier of my every need (Philippians 4:19), and now He was giving me the opportunity to prove Him.

"I cannot say that I was never in doubt as to whether I would end up without a partner at the end of the year. I did wonder, but I trusted God to take care of the law practice, since it was His anyway. However, I now had a peace in my heart that only comes when you know you are doing God's will.

"Any doubts I had were erased on December 31, 1979, when upon evaluating the books at the end of the year, there was only a $100 difference in our earnings. Since that date, I have led the firm in fees due to God's changing my image as a Divorce Trial Lawyer to a Damage Suit Trial Lawyer and Real Estate Lawyer. My associates and secretaries ask me, 'Where do you get all those cases?' God has so wonderfully blessed me (Ephesians 3:20), because I responded to His promptings and to His Word and took a stand regarding this Scriptural premise 'that God does not honor divorce.'

"Since my commitment to the Lord, God has allowed me to counsel over 200 couples not to file a divorce, but to honor God's Word and to love each other with no conditions attached, even as Jesus loves us. Many have accepted Christ as their own personal Lord and Savior as God's Word has been shared through spiritual counseling. I now view every appointment as an opportunity to explain that their problem is not legal, if seeking divorce, but it is spiritual."

Used by permission

Answers to Quiz 7

1-(h); 2-(i); 3-(a); 4-(g); 5-(b); 6-(c); 7-(f); 8-(d); 9-(e)

Personal Commitment and Accountability

In rebuilding the marriages of others with God's truth:

☐   1. I am commited to strengthening the marriages of others wherever possible.

☐   2. I purpose to direct my ministry through a local church that honors the Word of God.

☐   3. I purpose to be a consistent living example of a happy, fulfilled, victorious, and fruitful Christian.

☐   4. I purpose to develop a working knowledge of the principles and testimonies of the Bible relating to marriage, divorce, and remarriage.

☐   5. I have written out a clear and loving testimony about God's true and just standards of marriage.

☐   6. I purpose to explain the deception and destruction of today's "fairness theology" on divorce and remarriage to those who are considering divorce.

☐   7. I purpose to work at finding creative ways to strengthen failing marriages and families.

☐   8. I purpose to teach those who are already divorced or remarried how they can become effective rebuilders.

☐   9. I purpose to follow wise guidelines in avoiding the dangers in counseling others.

Signed＿＿＿＿＿＿＿＿＿＿＿＿＿＿＿＿＿ Date ＿＿＿＿＿＿

I, TOO, AM A REBUILDER . . .

Whenever you view the splendor of nature,
remember that the earth also is a "rebuilder."
It was created by God to perfection, but because
of sin, it was cursed. (See Genesis 1:31; 3:17.)
In God's mercy it was cleansed by the flood, and one day
it will be transformed in the presence of Christ.
(See Genesis 7:24; Revelation 21:1-5.)

Meanwhile, the earth has a living message for us.
Its mountains and oceans speak of God's majesty and power;
its mighty pines point us to God; its flowers and
grass remind us of how brief life on this earth really is.

THE EXCITING POTENTIAL OF REBUILDING

"Several years ago when your Rebuilder's supplement came out, I pored over it and studied it; but I just did not have the courage to implement those approaches because of the sensitivity of people in my church who had gone through a divorce. Just this past year, however, I decided I was going to try to follow the Scriptural principles as outlined in this supplement with a few selected couples.

"The first one whom I talked to was a young man who had divorced his wife. He was experiencing deep depression and turned to the church for help. One of my staff members led him to the Lord. What neither he nor I realized was that his former wife had taken back her maiden name, rededicated her life to the Lord, and joined the church about three weeks earlier. We placed the husband in a Sunday School class. Much to his surprise, the first morning he walked in, there was his former wife sitting across the room from him!

"As I continued working with this husband, I mentioned that God's will was that he put his marriage back together. He had never heard of such a thing in all his life. I handed him your Rebuilder's supplement. Now mind you, this was a brand new Christian with almost no Bible knowledge whatsoever. To make a long story short, he determined to re-establish his relationship with his former wife, following the steps outlined in your supplement. He and his wife began to see one another on a fairly regular basis. Then suddenly she gave him a letter at the end of one of their evenings. When he opened it, it informed him, 'What I prayed for these many years has finally happened. You have been saved, but it happened too late. I no longer love you.'

"Needless to say he was devastated. I reminded him of the principle of praying a protective hedge of thorns around his former wife. In about three weeks she contacted him and asked to see him. He called me immediately. He was very fearful that she was going to tell him that she was going to marry the other man in our church whom she was dating. I had no idea who the man was, but I suggested that maybe she wanted to talk about reconciliation. The husband could scarcely believe that because the other man had been sending her flowers and taking her out to fancy restaurants. However, when they met, his former wife told him that she wanted to return to him and restore their marriage.

"About two weeks later, another one of our men came to see me for counseling. He said he had just experienced the two roughest weeks of his life. He began to tell me how he had been dating this divorced woman in the church. These were the words he used: 'Without warning, in the midst of a growing and wonderful relationship that was about to result in an engagement, it was suddenly as if a wall went up around her, and I couldn't even get to her.'

"I laughed and told him what had happened. He said, 'I saw it with my own eyes—I saw it happen. I couldn't even get near her!' And then he asked, 'Could I have one of those supplements?' You see, his former wife is still in the church. I gave him your Rebuilder's supplement and asked him to study it and come back to see me the next week. When he returned the next week, he said, 'Pastor, did you know that divorce is wrong? I just didn't know that. I knew it was bad, but I didn't know it was a sin. I've sinned!' Again, to make a long story short, he was led to the Lord. His realization that he had violated God's will for his life is what God used to uncover the fact that he never really had been saved, even though he had been raised in the church all of his life.

"He is now in the process of applying the principles of that Rebuilder's supplement in an attempt to be reconciled with his wife. It's going to be extremely interesting to see what happens.

"In the meantime the first man and his former wife became engaged. They came to me for counseling, and I told them the story I just related about her former boyfriend. They were flabbergasted! I said to her, 'If you had married your boyfriend, you would have had another lost husband, but because you were obedient to the principles of God's Word, He used your obedience to bring that friend to Christ! He probably never would have realized his lost condition had he not gone through the deep depression and rejection that happened when you announced that you were returning to your husband.'

"This couple put their testimony in the local newspaper and invited the entire community to their wedding, which took place March 21, 1982. Their life message has already encouraged others, and we are beginning to see several broken marriages restored."

Used by permission

FURTHER NOTES AND INSIGHTS
ON REBUILDING

_____

_____

_____

_____

_____

_____

_____

_____

_____

_____

_____

_____

_____

_____

_____

_____

_____

_____

_____

_____

_____

_____

_____

_____

_____

_____